THE ACADEMIC STUDY OF RELIGION: 1975 PROCEEDINGS

and

PUBLIC SCHOOLS RELIGION-STUDIES: 1975 PROCEEDINGS

PREPRINTED PAPERS

FOR

THE ACADEMIC STUDY OF RELIGION SECTION

Compiled by

Anne Carr

and

THE PUBLIC SCHOOLS RELIGION-STUDIES GROUP

Compiled by

Nicholas Piediscalzi

AMERICAN ACADEMY OF RELIGION

ANNUAL MEETING

1975

Distributed by

SCHOLARS PRESS
University of Montana
Missoula, Montana 59801

THE ACADEMIC STUDY OF RELIGION: 1975

Compiled by
Anne Carr

PUBLIC SCHOOLS RELIGION-STUDIES: 1975

Compiled by
Nicholas Piediscalzi

Library of Congress Cataloging in Publication Data

American Academy of Religion. Academic Study of
    Religion Section.
    The academic study of religion.

    "Preprinted papers for the Academic Study of Re-
ligion Section, compiled by Anne Carr, and the
Public Schools Religion-Studies Group, compiled by
Nicholas Piediscalzi."
    Includes bibliographical references.
    1. Religion--Study and teaching--Congresses.
2. Religion in the public schools--Congresses.
I. Carr, Anne. II. Piediscalzi, Nicholas.
III. American Academy of Religion. Public Schools
Religion-Studies Group. IV. Title. V. Title:
Public schools religion studies.
BL41.A47 1975   200'.7   75-26653
ISBN 0-89130-023-6

Printing Department
University of Montana
Missoula, Montana 59801

TABLE OF CONTENTS

THE ACADEMIC STUDY OF RELIGION: 1975

THE MODEL FOR THE ACADEMIC STUDY OF RELIGION: MERE SCAFFOLDING OR IDOLATRY?

Gordon E. Pruett
Northeastern University

The study of religion rejoices in a seat at the academic round table. This status has been maintained recently largely on the strength of the claim of the history of religions as a discipline to an objective methodology. Thus, like chemistry and experimental psychology, the history of religions has a subject worthy of study (religious morphology) and methods by which to study it (sociological, psychological, historical-scientific, phenomenological). Moreover, as Clyde Holbrook has argued, in light of the humanistic significance of religious ideas, behavior and institutions no college of Liberal Arts without a Department of Religious Studies can call its curriculum complete.

The academic acceptance of religious studies was not the result of a prior recognition of its academic significance. On the contrary, it was the result of the convincing case made for the objectivity of religious studies, together with its recantation of the confessional stance. The history of religions presents a methodological stance of consummate academic respectability. It is concerned with the experience of the sacred, the perception an elucidation of human encounter with ultimate reality under all names. As long as it sticks to the job of describing the effects of experience and the causal flow of these effects, its credentials are impeccable. It cannot entirely ignore the transcendent dimension itself, of course. Thus we hear mention made of the sacred, the transcendent, ultimate reality, meaning, and so forth. Now these are terms to indicate in the most abstract and remote manner possible that which is assumed to be the first cause in the history of religion. However, once we begin to struggle with the sacred in history we move (as it seems we must) completely into the humanistic plane. That is to say, transcendence is equated with its manifestation in the history of religions to all intents and purposes. Thus we arrive at the study of religious phenomena. This is another way of saying that we study what seems to be (1) religious and (2) academically admissible, both at the same time.

Peter Berger (JSSR Autumn 1974) has suggested recently that while the bracketing of the gods is legitimate and necessary to the scientific study of religion (and by implication to its academic status), there is some danger that in so bracketing we exclude the transcendent nature of religious causality from our understanding. The effect is the failure to understand the "real cause" of religious behavior, and to "level out" our dimensions of understanding and interpretation, to limit religious life to that which we can measure and quantify. Berger makes these points as a corrective to a too facile acceptance of the dominance of the secular in the world we know.

I emphasize them to show that a "scientific" methodology inevitably precludes understanding of more than the given. If we know anything about the history of religion, we know that it may not be reduced to explication of the given. There are too many Luthers, Ramanujas and Mertons to allow such a conclusion. What Berger perceives in his discomfort is that (to use the terms of Wilfred Cantwell Smith) we cannot understand tradition without faith any better than we can understand faith without tradition.

At this point I should discuss the epistemological crisis of the academic study of religion as I see it, namely the problem of objectivity. Before doing so, however, I would like to suggest what perhaps the real implications are for the presence of religious studies in the academic curriculum. Robert Bellah indicated in his essay in the report of the Undergraduate Study of Religion (Welch, 1972) that there _is_ cause for concern on the part of secular universities about the presence of religious studies in their midst. For the ultimate goal of religious studies lies beyond methodology, in truth, in the integrity of the entire quest of human understanding. Religious studies, and especially history of religions, possess several obvious characteristics which indicate that their "success" is not to be assessed in methodological terms. The _first_ is the universality in time and space of its scope. One simply cannot ignore the "religious dimension" of collective and individual life at any level, time, or place. This is true not only for the socio-economic and socio-psychological but of the artistic, for example. The "nature and essence" of art is so obviously indebted to religious perceptions and the quest for religious meaning that it would be patently absurd to claim an understanding of art that was oblivious to religious concerns.

Second, the nature of the concerns and questions which arise in this grand spectrum is as peculiar as the scope itself. It is obvious in the works of the grand masters of the history and/or phenomenology of religion (Kristensen, Eliade, Kitagawa, Van der Leeuw, E. O. James, Otto, et.al.) that what the history of religion wishes to understand is the nature of being, reality itself, the transcendent, the sacred throughout human experience. It may be objected that a great deal of work in the history of religions focuses upon particular groups and individuals working out their lives in their own context, e.g. Parsis in Bombay, Zunis in New Mexico, Aos in Nagaland, Jews in Russia, Shi'ites in Iran, etc. But it seems clear that such studies (and such endeavors) must participate in an attempt to grasp consciously, sympathetically, the human whence and whither, its tragedy and its destiny, as a whole, if they are to succeed.

The _third_ characteristic of the history of religions is very briefly described. It is the fusion of the first two in the person and work of the historian. That is, the historian of religions who can really do his or her job is one whose range of interests and attributes is potentially universal, and whose concerns are ultimate. I do not think that such a self-understanding is as apt and necessary anywhere as it is in the historian of religions (nor are humility and maturity more indispensable).

Now in light of these unique characteristics (and perhaps others that should be added) religious studies, and the history of religions, stand apart from the other disciplines because, to use the nice slang expression, they put it all together. In this respect the history of religions is (in the sense of ought to be) an anti-methodology. The religious perspective is the perspective on the ultimate meaning of all those areas of humane endeavor with which the academy is concerned. Religious studies are studies to which all other humanistic disciplines must turn for the integrating view, the context in which they work. No university is a _university_ without religious and history of religions--or better, the history of human stabs at truth and goodness. I suppose then that religious studies threatens the academic fiefdoms called departments or colleges. And if so, then the secular university which is committed to method has a right to feel threatened.

A second major problematic here is the old chestnut, the objective study of religion. Especially noteworthy are the phenomenology of religion and the study of religious symbols.

In order to qualify as a discipline, religious studies and the history of religions must have a methodology, a manner of studying agreed-upon data which is independent of the cares of the student. Methodology guarantees objectivity. The phenomenology of religion and the study of religious symbols exemplify the priority of methodology. Phenomenology is represented as a philosophical method which may be applied to any phenomena. Armed with epoche and eidetic vision, the scholar may elucidate a situation or context as it "is", i.e. as it appears. What is significant here is the fact that in order to do this one must suspend the question of ultimate meaning, or transcendence. In the case of religious phenomenology, one describes the religious condition of man--and nothing more.

What we have learned as a result is how things appear. We learn by virtue of suspending concerns and doubts--especially doubts--about things being what they seem to be. These doubts are not only epistemological but moral and--yes--religious. It may be that, say, Kiekegaard's thoughts on the subject of doubting cannot be taught or rendered more conveniently for the task of religionswissenschaft. But they cannot, to my way of thinking, simply be ignored in order to achieve a consistent method. Husserl was quite perceptive in his revival of Descartes. Both wanted a method by which doubt could be circumvented. Indeed, the prime prerequisite for method is precisely the circumvention of doubt.

But how may such maneuvering help us to understand, say, the concept of Maya, rites of sanctification, or the doctrine of prevenient grace, all of which presuppose a radical kind of doubt? Perhaps by suspending our own personal doubting in order to observe the doubting of others. The "existential" doubt or "anxiety" now becomes an object of study, understanding of which is precluded by a method which (in order to succeed) cuts off any sympathetic reverberations of that doubt in our own lives and experience.

Something is wrong here--and what is wrong is that in order to gain an objective, disciplined, understanding we have suspended our own participation in the "phenomenon" we choose to observe. I am suggesting that unless we encourage interaction between our own doubtings and those so obviously present in our "data", our understanding of this religious dimension is incomplete and corrupted. Yet the phenomenological epoche seems to prevent such understanding from the start, as a methodological prerequisite. There are other areas where the same comments would be appropriate, such as the question of hope.

The development of symbology is also important in this context. Certainly the recognition that the religious life of people beyond our acquaintance and culture was not an inferior striving but a legitimate grasp of meaning is the cornerstone of the history of religions. The conceptual means for understanding that life depends in part on the notion of symbol. Jung, Eliade and many others have released us from the bonds of chauvinism here, at least as far as our intellects are concerned. But their success has a price. It is necessary to remove the elements, expressions, and forms of the religious life of others

from their full context and place them in a kind of neutral space ("as symbols").
This neutralization allows us to study the religions "themselves", their expressions and symbols, and find there meaning, relevance and insight. Moreover,
the symbolic morphologist finds that symbols may be arranged in categories, and
that their meanings are more or less fixed despite various permutations (e.g. the
axis mundi, the self). Thus despite the enormous flexibility in interpretation
achieved by the study of symbols, we are still dealing with an objectivization
of human experience, for the sake of a disciplined and objective "understanding."

A way out of this dilemma is suggested in the idea of experiential simulation, or the recovery of religious experience by imitation. Here a more profound level of understanding can emerge from the imitation of (I) the symbolic
(ritual) actions and (II) the "religious experience" of whatever religious group
occupies our attention. Perhaps, one might argue, if one adopts the lotus position, disciplines oneself in the art/skill of meditation, or follows prescribed
ascetic practices one may enter samadhi, pass through the gate of death, or cross
the narrow bridge. At least one will have gained a sympathetic understanding of
the rites and experience of the people who undergo them. The theory seems to be
that inherent in the actions themselves is the power to transform, so that who-
soever will may come.

As an advance on the intellectualist approach to understanding simulation
of religious experience has much to offer. It might put one in touch with feelings,
not just doctrinal pronouncements. But let us recognize that it is a method; and
that it owes much to the rationale of the laboratory experiment. An experiment
is valuable insofar as it can be repeated by different technicans under the same
conditions. The assumption (presumption) of the experimental technique is that
there is something inherent in the exchange of interaction (i.e. "in the world")
which operates independently of human participation. Thus in simulating religious
rites or disciplines or experiences in order to gain understanding one assumes
that the pwoer of transformation is in the rite, rather than in the person, or
in the dynamic of person and rite. If the former assumption is correct, then a
particular rite, such as the investment of the Brahmin boy with the threestranded
cord (Upanayana) will mean the same thing, provide the same fundamental insights,
not only to every Brahmin, but to anyone who undergoes the rite. This conclusion
is questionable not only with reference to a westerner who might pass through to
adulthood in this way (an impossible situation), but with reference to any rite
within one's own tradition. While I have more respect for the doctrine of opus
operatum than I used to, I do not think that it should be used as a methodological
principle.

A probable rejoiner would be that like all rites of passage this one
reflects the distinction between the sacred and the profane, or the transsection
of sacred time, or is an example of the myth of the eternal return. Thus its
meaning is the same as all other such rites and myths. Therefore I could draw
upon rites I do not understand to gain insight into the one I do not. But what
I am told is that the rite participates in a body or species of phenomena. What
I am concerned with is not its classification, facility with which is prerequisite
of understanding, but the rit's fundamental import. Even if I were absolutely
clear on what "sacred and profane", "myth of the eternal return", or "transsection
of sacred time" meant, I would not be clear on what the rite meant to anyone, but
rather on the category of interpretation designated by these generalizations.
Should I discard these morphological terms, I am still left with the difference
between the Brahmacarya rite and, say, that of Baptism. The former I do not
understand, the latter I think I do, and that seems to be the end of it. Simulation will not help, or so it seems to me.

Finally, I come to a conceptualization of the meaning and end of the history of religions that seems to me fruitful and more honest intellectually. Three stories will help to illustrate my view. The first is told by Chuang Tzu.

> Once when Hsi Shih, the most beautiful of women, was frowning and beating her breast, an ugly woman saw her and thought, "now I have found out how to become beautiful!" So she went home to her village and did nothing but frown and beat her breast. When the rich men of the village saw her, they bolted themselves into their houses and dared not come out; when the poor people of the village saw her they took wife and child by the hand and ran at top speed. This woman had seen that someone frowning was beautiful and thought that she had only to frown in order to become beautiful.

As a critique of the decisiveness of method, the story requires no further elaboration.

Second, you may recall a television series called The Prisoner, in which (after the requisite number of adventures) the prisoner realizes his ambition of discovering who the chief jailer is: "Number one, who is number one?" he asks again and again. The last episode of the series reveals the identity of number one as the prisoner himself. The story of the prisoner reminds me of the real goal of the history of religions. As the prisoner conducts an ingenious and vigorous search for his elusive self-understanding, he does not know that it is himself he searches for until the search is successful--indeed, that is precisely the (very unexpected!) mark of the story's end. His "method" was appropriate to his end in the most ironical way only.

The third story has a related point. It is the Hassidic tale of Eisik son of Jekel which concludes Eliade's Myths, Dreams and Mysteries as well as Heinrich Zimmer's Myths and Symbols in Indian Art and Civilization. Following advice given in a dream, Eisik journeys from his home in Cracow to Prague to search for gold said to be buried under a bridge. A Christian officer guarding the bridge learned of Eisik's quest, and (laughing) recounted a dream of his own in which he was told to look in the kitchen of one Eisik son of Jekel in Cracow. The guard took no notice. Eisik, on the other hand, hurried home and found a great treasure in his kitchen. In the case of the prisoner, one searches, perhaps unwittingly, for oneself. In the Hassidic tale, a second element is added--that it is necessary to depart from home in some sense, without complete certainty as to what you will find.

A number of topics for investigation arise from this. I want to focus on the two that seem most significant. First, the purpose of the history of religions is to understand persons, not religions. As I have already implied, I do not believe that objects have meaning in themselves, even religious objects (or especially religious objects); and that conclusion holds for those weird methodological constructs "religions", the even more weird construct called "religion", and for any rite, belief, or norm found within their boundaries. As Wilfred Cantell Smith has said, We must concern ourselves with what ritual and tradition do to and for a person, rather than with the question of whether they are meaningful in themselves. In short, the history of religions really ought to be concerned with the human condition as persons have endured or enjoyed it, not with the theme and variation of dynamism, animism, power, sacred and profane, or what have you.

Second, the persons involved include us. It is more than a little hard
to believe that we have tried diligently to understand others without any serious
attempt to understand ourselves at the same time. Of course the latter end seemed
so unacademic, so subjective. The journey which the history of religions represents is our journey; and at the end of it, or somewhere along the way, we find
ourselves. I am certain that Zimmer is right, that it is true that one cannot
find one-self unless one goes out in search--even, like the prisoner, unwittingly.
One must be told the truth (without preparation, and as the most incredible of
surprises) by someone who is other in all senses of the term, cultural, psychological, etc.

I argue, then, the true calling of the history of religions is self-
understanding by virtue of encounter with the other. But I hasten to add that
the encounter is not merely a trick by which the hidden secrets are revealed,
like a combination for a safe. Rather, self-understanding incorporates understanding of the other. In this regard it seems very difficult to improve on
Smith's agenda for the history of religions. Its task is symbolized by a progression from speaking of an "it" to speaking of "they" to "we talking about
them". This may become "that 'we' talk with 'you'." The culmination of this
progression is when "we all are talking with each other about 'us'." In other
words, the task of the history of religions is to help create the global community through the mutually dependent acts of understanding the other and
understanding ourselves. Moreover, this agenda describes a dynamic process
rather than a "misplaced concretion" a la Whitehead. For mutual understanding
is in part, at least, a function of the historical, fluctuating nature of the
human condition. This "method" refers to nothing but itself, and therefore
ceases to be a method at all.

CONFUCIUS AS ZEN MASTER:
ON MARRYING CONTENT AND
METHOD IN TEACHING

Jeffrey F. Meyer
University of North Carolina
at Charlotte

The spirit of Zen Buddhism and Confucianism would no doubt
be considered by most students of Asia as antipodal. My paper is not
conceived so much as a challenge to that view as an exploration of the
intricate relationship of dependency between the two. This dependency
results in a coincidence of purpose and aspiration in certain areas
which I would like to propose for your consideration.

To current American sentiment, chiefly perhaps in the
"counterculture," Confucius is stereotyped as the proponent of order
and heirarchy, of conformity to precedent. He is seen as the unremitting moralist, at his worst a humourless purveyor of dismal platitudes,
and a stuffy pedant who advocates every type of conventional behavior.
Zen, by contrast, is inevitably typed as the breath of fresh air,
individualistic, mystical, a-moral, encouraging freedom, naturalness
and spontaneity.

We cannot stop now to consider the reasons for these unfor-
tunate stereotypes, which have their sources as much in ancient China
as in the conditions of our contemporary culture. Yet even if one
sees the descriptions given above as the exaggerations they are, one
would still think that Zen and Confucianism would find themselves at
odds wherever they came into contact. Yet that is not the case. Even
such an advocate of freedom from convention as Alan Watts pointed out
long ago that "since the Sung dynasty (959-1278 A.D.) Zen has consistently fostered Confucianism and was the main source of the introduction of its principles into Japan,"[1] seeing in Confucianism a necessary
element in its own program. How is this to be explained?

It is possible to line up a whole series of statements which
will erode the stereotypes of Zen and Confucianism stated above.
Many Westerners have gone to Japan seeking freedom and spontaneity
only to discover an extremely rigid discipline awaiting them. "The
constant supervision of the master throughout the course of this study
assures that the student's own personal views and his mistaken and
deluded notions are discarded one by one, for, in order to pass a koan,
he must reach the traditionally correct understanding of it. No
other understanding is acceptable or accepted.[2]

As to Zen's being a-moral, former beat poet Gary Snyder remarks, "I've never known anybody who did anything particularly irresponsible or justified anything he did whatsoever on the basis of Zen--
ever. The danger of Zen is not that people become moral anarchists--
it's quite the opposite. It's that they become complete supporters of
whatever establishment is around. That's the real moral anarchism of
Zen."[3]

The student who comes to Zen looking for mystical insights
is instead given the harsh regimen of the kondo (meditation hall) with

7

its back breaking postures, its hours of silent meditation and occa-
sional sermons which most often inculcate, as R. H. Blyth discovered,
two lofty principles: "don't smoke while pissing, and answer '<u>Oi</u>'
immediately with '<u>hai</u>'" (Japanese formula of greeting).[4]

The foregoing remarks do not demolish the stereotypes mentioned at the beginning. They are meant only to fill out a very
partial picture, for Zen is indeed a way of liberation and spontaneity.
They serve to point out that the achievement of Zen is rather more
complex than one expects at the outset, in most cases the culmination
of a long and arduous process.[5] They also suggest that Zen requires a
certain social context as matrix out of which it can effectively function, that it is in fact a way of liberation for those who have already
accepted the discipline of social convention. "(Zen) must be seen
against the background of societies regulated by the principles of
Confucianism, with their heavy stress on propriety and punctilious
ritual."[6] We are thus confronted with the anomaly that Zen requires
Confucianism (or conventionality) and if it does not have it, must
provide its own brand of conventional discipline before pointing out
the escape route of liberation. This is why in Japan, Zen monasteries
have often become training schools for boys. If this seems like a
case of hitting skulls with hammers so that it will feel good when
the pounding ceases, it is not. It is rather the application of a
sound developmental and educational insight that the difficult part
of the process in absolutely essential if it is to succeed, a point to
which I would like to return at the end of this paper.

Having shown that Zen requires a great amount of "Confucian"
discipline and a matrix of the conventional out of which to operate,
we must now ask whether Confucianism has any elements of "Zen" in it.
In the following discussion I intend to be quite restrictive, limiting
the subject of my observations to the Confucius who appears in the
<u>Analects</u>.[7] I doubt that I could make my point in regard to <u>Confucians</u>
generally, unless it be possible with the Ch'an and Taoist influenced
Neo-Confucians of the Ming Dynasty. My assertion is that Confucius
was a Zen master in the sense that he taught a discipline which leads
to a perfection expressed in freedom and spontaniety. Other dissimi-
larities, such as the lack of anything like an enlightenment experience (<u>satori</u>), I must simply ignore.

There are first of all a number of superficial similarities
between the behavior of Confucius and that of a Zen Master. The
stereotype of a flat-footed moralizer quickly disappears in a careful
reading of the <u>Analects</u>. More often than not, the Master's answers
to queries are quite original and unexpected, his judgments are stimulating. His responses are sometimes humorous, sometimes brusque, and
once he is reported to have rapped a young man across the shins with
a stick in fine Zen style.[8] When his favorite disciple Yen Hui died
Confucius was reproached by his followers for "wailing without restraint," but he did not repent of it. One is reminded that the Zen
Master Hakuin was deeply disturbed when he heard that Zen Master
Yen-t'ou screamed at the top of his voice when murdered by a robber.
Only later did he realize that this wail was just as perfect in its
spontaneity as the silence of Abbot Kawaisen and his monks who allowed
themselves to be burned alive by soldiers as they sat calmly in <u>zazen</u>
(meditation posture).[9]

To go on to more substantial matters, I would like to call attention to the use of a single but important term in the <u>Analects</u>, jen 仁, variously translated as Goodness, Humanity, Love, Benevolence, Virtue, Human-heartedness, Manhood, Manhood-at-Its-Best, and so forth.[10] None of these translations do it justice, since they allow it to fall into the slot of generalized virtue in our minds. In proposing this <u>jen</u>, Confucius seems to tell us no more than to "be good" "be virtuous" etc., and thus the stereotype of the banal moralizing of Confucius. But the very number and variety of translations ought to alert us to the fact that we are dealing with an important and difficult concept. As soon as we pass on to an examination of the usage of the term <u>jen</u> in the <u>Analects</u>, it becomes obvious how mysterious and elusive the concept is.

<u>Jen</u> is first of all a human quality, though it would appear to be at the very summit of human perfection. The highest appellation for a person found in the <u>Analects</u> is <u>sheng jen</u> 聖人,[11] divine sage, and applies to such figures as Yao, Shun and Yü, who are nearly divinized Sage Emperors of the past. <u>Jen</u>, on the other hand, is a possible though difficult attainment for living mortals. It appears to be superior even to, or perhaps the highest accomplishment of, the chün tzu 君子, or "gentlemen" (another vapid translation in the light of modern connotations).[12] Thus <u>jen</u> is the crown of human accomplishment.

But if we look for a precise definition of <u>jen</u> in the <u>Analects</u>, we will be disappointed. Confucius was singularly unwilling to be pinned down on the subject. "The Master seldom spoke of profit, fate or Goodness (<u>jen</u>)." Or again, when asked about <u>jen</u>, the Master responds with a play on words: "The Good (<u>jen</u>) man is chary (<u>jen</u>) of speech. Ssu-ma Niu said, So that is what is meant by Goodness--to be chary of speech? The Master said, Seeing that the doing of it is so difficult, how can one be otherwise than chary of talking about it?"[13] One immediately feels that Confucius' evasiveness about <u>jen</u> is cautiousness in the face of a mystery rather than a perverse delight in mystification. It is the same reluctance one sees in other spiritual leaders such as Buddha or Jesus to <u>talk</u> about, much less define, the inexpressible.

We find a similar relectance on the part of the Master to say that any particular individual of his acquaintance was <u>jen</u>. "Someone said, Jan Yung is Good (<u>jen</u>), but he is a poor talker. The Master said, What need has he to be a good talker? Those who down others with claptrap are seldom popular. Whether he is Good, I do not know. But I see no need for him to be a good talker."[14] Again and again in the <u>Analects</u>, the example of some individual is proposed for discussion, Confucius and/or his disciples accord them high praise for some great virtue or accomplishment, yet the Master always recoils from saying that the person is <u>jen</u>: "Of the saying 'He upon whom neither love of mastery, vanity, resentment nor covetousness have any hold may be called Good,' the Master said, Such a one has done what is difficult, but whether he should be called Good (<u>jen</u>) I do not know."[15] Here too, Confucius' evasiveness seems to stem from an appreciation of the interiority and spiritual nature of <u>jen</u>, affirming in other words that there is no exterior pattern of conduct that can certify the subject's being <u>jen</u>.

We also have much testimony in the <u>Analects</u> of the difficulty of "doing" <u>jen</u>. "The Master said, I for my part have never yet seen one who really cared for Goodness, nor one who really abhorred wickedness. One who really cared for Goodness would never let any other consideration come first. . . . Has anyone ever managed to do Good with his whole might even as long as the space of a single day? I think not."[16] There is also Confucius' statement that the true "Knight of the Way" must be stout of heart because he has a long journey before him and a heavy burden to bear, and the burden is <u>jen</u>. "Must we not grant that it is a heavy one to bear? Only with death does his journey end; then must we not grant that he has far to go?"[17]

Finally, I would like to cite two passages which lead us right to the heart of the paradox of <u>jen</u>. A disciple asks about the meaning of <u>jen</u>, and as usual, Confucius avoids any direct definition, but remarks: "Jen cannot be obtained till what is difficult has been duly done. He who has done this may be called Good."[18] Juxtaposed to this statement, we have Confucius saying: "Is Goodness indeed so far away? If we really wanted Goodness, we should find that it was at our very side."[19] The first statement emphasizes the difficulty of attainment which has already been amply documented. The second statement suggests that <u>jen</u> is immediate, automatic, present at the snap of the fingers. But because it is obvious that <u>jen</u> is the highest attainment, we are forced to see these two statements not as inconsistancies but as two stages of a process in which the first presents almost insurmountable difficulties and the second the ease of mastery.

We may find some support for this argument in two passages in the <u>Analects</u> where Confucius describes <u>jen</u> negatively.[20] The passages are nearly identical, both asserting that the truly wise man can never be perplexed, the brave can never be afriad, and the Good (<u>jen</u>) can never be unhappy (yu 憂). Yu has a number of meanings: sad, anxious, troubled, worried, melancholy, mournful. Both passages employ parallelism, so that I think we may infer that since the first two members are opposites (brave-afraid, wise-perplexed), so <u>jen</u> is conceived as the direct opposite of yu. The state of <u>jen</u> may therefore be seen as one which includes some kind of confidence, serenity and joy, and which would exclude the sort of self-reflection and questioning which lead to doubt, worry and anxiety. We recall that for Confucius, to prefer (好hao) something is better than to know (知 chih) it, but to delight (樂 le) in it is better than merely to prefer it.[21] The joy of <u>jen</u> is descriptive of the state of a man so wrapped up in his task that all consciousness of effort is forgotten. Once an adventurer asked a disciple what kind of man Confucius was. The disciple did not answer him and when the incident was reported to the Master, he said, Why didn't you say: he is "so intent on enlightening the eager that he forgets his hunger, and so happy in doing so that he forgets the bitterness of his lot (yu) and does not realize that old age is at hand."[22] The anecdote points to the same unselfconscious involvement, spontaneous participation in the task.

I think we can now summarize our knowledge of <u>jen</u> so far. It is a human quality, but lofty enough that its nature defies exact definition and its presence in an individual cannot be verified by any external signs. Once achieved however, all strain and effort which were required in the process of acquisition, fall away.

As described, the process leading to jen has a certain commonplace ring of truth about it. It is an every day human experience that hard practice leads to the ease of mastery, as everyone who has learned to ride a bicycle, shoot a basket or swing a golf club will testify. But what is true at the merely physical level, can be verified at the summit of probably every great religious tradition. Those who have read Eugen Herrigel's Zen and the Art of Archery will recall that it took the author five years of frustration and pain in learning to master the art (both physical and spiritual) which then became so simple as to defy belief.[23] The achievement of satori may be seen to follow a similar pattern, particularly in the Rinzai school where koans must be mastered which require unremitting effort and lead to utter frustration on the part of the student before the flash of awakening comes. Afterwards, all becomes easy. In Christianity, Augustine's "love and do what you will" and Luther's "sin boldly" are not norms for catechetics, but states of soul which come at the end of a long and arduous journey.

The state of perfection which these statements describe is marked by effortlessness and spontaniety. It also includes a trans-ethical component which is exactly what impells outside observers to fret about Zen's "a-morality," or the a-morality of Christian, Muslim or Buddhist mystics. It is in his allusions to the achievement of jen that Confucius comes closest to this perspective. One of the few auto-biographical passages of the Analects says:

The Master said, At fifteen I set my heart upon learning. At thirty, I had planted my feet firm upon the ground. At forty, I no longer suffered from perplexities. At fifty, I knew what were the biddings of Heaven. At sixty, I heard them with docile ear. At seventy, I could follow the dictates of my own heart; for what I desired no longer overstepped the boundaries of right.[24]

At seventy, Confucius had transcended morality and achieved spontaneity.

I believe that Fingarette is correct in maintaining that jen must be understood in relationship to the other key Confucian concept of li (禮 ritual), though a discussion of this would take us too far afield. Let me just say that the two concepts are the reverse sides of the same coin, li referring to the external standards of conduct and human relationships, jen focusing on the personal quality of one who has thoroughly mastered li. The perfection of li leads not to a soulless mechanical correctness but to a mastery which permits spontaniety, but as in the case of jen, only at the highest level of attainment. One may use the analogy of music. Only the performing artist who has thoroughly mastered a musical score can move beyond rote performance to interpretation, the nuances of personal contribution being possible only when he has the ability to execute a piece with mechanical perfection. The comparison is suggested by Confucius' own emphasis on the analogous concepts of li and yüeh (music). The music of the ancients, he said, "insofar as one can find out about it began with a strict unison. Soon the musicians were given more liberty; but the tone remained harmonious, brilliant, consistent, right on till the close."[25]

12

Practical Postscript for Teachers

Social critics today worry a good deal about "the breakdown
of morality," "ethical vacuums" and so forth. In this context, talk
of the "a-morality" of Zen and the trans-ethical, spontaneous level of
Confucian perfection may seem an ill-timed emphasis. As I have indicated there is little danger of negative influence if the traditions
are correctly understood, for there is no rejection of, rather a trans-
cending of, ethics and morality. But because of the nature of our own
culture, so antithetical to oriental and traditional cultures in its
glorification of the individual and his freedom, there is a real possibility of misapprehension. As teachers we are much less circumspect
than the "masters" in our handling of the mystery of this state of
moral transcendence and spontaneity. We too readily point to the mystic
realization, to the utter freedom of the fully realized man, and fail
to emphasize the long and arduous path which is its precondition in all
the great religious traditions. Students respond predictably well to
the lure of freedom but usually make a short circuit in seeking it without the traditional route of discipline, and misunderstand the religious
traditions in the process. Zen and Confucius' way do hold the promise
of freedom and spontaneity, as we have seen, but I suspect it ought
never to be looked at as a goal, but a by-product.

I think that the tendency to short circuit can be detected in
a number of areas. One would be that of logical versus intuitive
thought, and again, we all realize that we live in an age that has come
to suspect the pretensions of the intellect, so the short circuit is
easy. Even such a seasoned scholar as D.T. Suzuki encourages it with
statements like "Logic has so intimidated us that we shrink and shiver
whenever its name is mentioned."[26] What Dr. Suzuki does not know is
that most of his readership, if my students are any indication, not
only does not shiver at the mention of logic, they do not know what
it is. Or again, Suzuki discusses the saying, "Empty handed I go, and
behold the space is in my hands!" and says:

> By this we are made perfectly happy, for strangely this con-
> tradiction is what we have been seeking for all the time ever
> since the dawning of the intellect. The dawning of the
> intellect did not mean the assertion of the intellect but
> the transcending of itself. The meaning of the proposition
> "A is A" is realized only when "A is not-A." To be itself
> is not to be itself--this is the logic of Zen, and satisfies
> all our aspirations.[27]

My point is that until we have probed the long and hard road of logic
and rational thought and discovered to our distress its limitations,
Zen's logic will be a short circuit and not satisfy all over aspirations.

Just as the pre-logically trained mind cannot make the jump
to the supralogical, so the person of small moral sensitivity can in no
way be "liberated" by a trans-moral approach. My own feeling is that
the mystical, trans-moral level of attainment cannot be "taught" at
all, only indicated obliquely with the reserve of a Confucius who
refused to define jen and refused to even name the models who had
attained it. We who simply try to teach it as part of an academic
discipline focused on understanding in the broadest sense, need to be

just as circumspect. Furthermore, I doubt that it can be directly
taught because teaching implies making something part of the intellectual and experiential property of a community of inquirers. But the
mystical, trans-moral achievement we have been discussing can never,
I think be a communal social phenomenon. It remains always personal,
individual and interior. There are no direct "methods" for attaining
it, no certification of its authenticity by any public tribunal. It
is self-authenticated, and we observers stand before it as before a
mystery.

     There are a number of other ways of formulating the problem
we have been discussing. It is the difference between being a guru
and a teacher, between imparting experiential realization or understanding, or to use much older terms, between the search for wisdom
(sapientia) and knowledge (scientia). The temptation to be or do the
first in these three pairs of alternatives can be very strong, for my
ego at least likes to think that it has a bit of superior wisdom to
impart. But there lies the danger. I am not a guru and if Confucius
is correct in his approach, then I would not be freeing a student if
I allow him to make the short circuit, but rather shackling him to ways
of thinking or behavior patterns that he is not yet ready to personally
appropriate.

     Nevertheless, I am not completely content to rest with the
cautionary points I have just suggested. There is a difference, I
believe, between teaching Zen and say, the History of Buddhism
(Christianity, Islam, etc.) Something of the very essence of Zen mocks
the standard academic approach to teaching a content oriented course.
Zen calls into question the intellectual enterprise itself. At this
point, the teacher of Zen may try to solve the problem by ascending to
the next level of intellectuality and talking about the fact that Zen
cannot really be talked about. I hope that a more integral solution
may be found and would suggest that as a topic which needs to be discussed.

     By way of conclusion I would like to suggest the following
questions as possible ways of formulating the problem for discussion:

     1) Is there an element of the supra-rational, supra-
         moral in every great religious tradition and if
         so, how does one "teach" it?

     2) What is the difference between teaching this element
         as a spiritual attainment and teaching it in an academic
         course? Is there some middle ground between religious
         training and a purely intellectual approach?

     3) More generally, is there a way to marry content with
         method in teaching a religious expression which is
         supra-rational, supre-moral?

     Stated in these terms, the paradoxical nature of the task be-
comes clear. How do we teach, in an academic, intellectual setting, a
discipline or religion which scorns academia and intellectuality as the
greatest source of illusion?

14

1. Alan Watts, The Way of Zen (N. Y.: Vintage Books, 1957), p.148.

2. Ruth Fuller Sasaki, in Nancy Wilson Ross, The World of Zen (N. Y.: Vintage Books, 1960), p. 25.

3. In Dom Aelred Graham, Conversations: Christian and Buddhist (N. Y.: Harvest Book, 1968), p. 61.

4. R. H. Blyth, Zen in English Literature and Oriental Classics (Tokyo: Hokuseido Press, 1942), p. 21.

5. The example of Hakuin immediately comes to mind. One can see the slow and agonizing process of his enlightenment outlined in Heinrich Dumoulin, A History of Zen Buddhism (Boston: Beacon Press, 1963), pp. 242-68.

6. Watts, p. 143.

7. For purposes of comparison, I am using the Ho Yen edition of the Lun Yü in Hsiao Ching Lun Yü Chi Chüeh 孝經·論語集解 , published by the Hsin Hsing Shu Chü, (Taipei: 1970); James Legge, the Confucian Analects, in The Four Books (Taiwan reprint by Wen Hsing Shu Tien, Taipei: 1964); Arthur Waley, The Analects of Confucius (N. Y.: Vintage Book reprint of 1938 Allen & Unwin edition).

8. XIV, 46. The translations in the paper are from Waley unless otherwise noted.

9. XI, 9.

10. Watts, p. 135.

11. Waley's translation for jen is Good or Goodness, so that is the form which will be used in this paper. In this discussion of jen I must express my debt to the analysis in Herbert Fingarette, Confucius--the Secular as Sacred (New York: Harper Torchbooks, 1972), pp. 37ff.

12. VI, 28; VII, 33.

13. XIV, 7.

14. IX, 1; XII, 3. Waley notes that Confucius reluctance to speak of jen's meaning is a result of Ssu-ma Niu's inability to comprehend the "mystery" of jen. Cf. ft. nt. 2, p. 163.

15. V, 4.

16. XIV, 2; see also V, 7 & 18.

17. IV, 6.

18. VIII, 7.

19. VI, 20. 仁者先難而後獲 可謂仁 The word huo 獲 here is quite descriptive, having the literal meaning to "catch" or "seize" in hunting, then the more general significance of obtaining something. One first goes through that which is difficult, then gets it.

20. VII, 29. 仁遠乎哉．我欲仁斯仁至矣. An alternative translation to Waley's would be something like the following: "Is _jen_ far off? I desire it and it is immediately there!"

21. IX, 28; XIV, 30.

22. VI, 18.

23. VII, 18.

24. Eugen Herrigel, <u>Zen in the Art of Archery</u> (N. Y.: Vintage Books, 1971, p.88.

25. II, 4. In another place, Confucius is describing the conduct of two groups of men whose conduct differed, though in both cases was worthy of approbation. He concludes with a personal reference: "As for me, I am different from any of these. I have no 'thou shalt' and no 'thou shalt not.' (XVIII, 8.) 我則異於是．無可無不可. The final phrase is cryptic, thus Legge translates "I have no course for which I am pre-determined, and no course against which I am pre-determined," which seems to indicate that there is no external norm which can of itself be judged right.

26. III, 23.

THE PLACE OF THEOLOGY WITHIN RELIGIOUS STUDIES

Paul G. Wiebe
Wichita State University

I

At first glance, the right of theology[1] to exist within the recently constructed religious studies programs appears to be beyond dispute. Certainly theology is a religious phenomenon which, like other phenomena such as myth, ritual, scripture, and religious association, deserves objective scrutiny. The historical investigation of the theological reflections of Shankara, Nagarjuna, Augustine, Maimonides, and al-Ashari is as important to an understanding of religion as are the studies of cosmogonic myths, initiation rituals, oral traditions and their transformations into authoritative writings, and forms of religious communions.

A problem emerges, however, when both the institutional framework and the nature of the two--theology and religious studies--are considered. Theology is that discipline which articulates the doctrines of a particular religious community; therefore, the institutional framework within which the theologian thinks and speaks is just this positive community. On the other hand, religious studies programs are located within the pluralistic context of the secular, often public, university. So where theology serves the needs of a specific group, religious studies serve a religiously neutral society and thus seek to be free from any special interests. The contrast in institutional frameworks, then, is one between particular religious community and pluralistic society, and so between seminary and university. And alongside this contrast lies the one between the natures of the two enterprises: for religious studies programs often attempt to be descriptive in their approach, largely because of their sensitivity to their pluralistic context; but the very significance of theology is that it is a prescriptive, or normative, discipline. That is to say, while religious studies seek to describe how people have been, and are, religious, the task of theology is to prescribe how people ought to be religious. These contrasts raise the question of whether theology, as a normative discipline native to a seminary, can appropriately be placed within the program of religious studies in a secular, pluralistic university. Does not the very conception of secular religious studies preclude the theological enterprise?

It is my contention that theology has a legitimate and necessary position within the religious studies curriculum. But the "theology" which belongs in the study of religion is not the traditional systematic theology of the seminary curriculum; it is, rather, a theology reconceived along lines appropriate to the pluralistic context of the contemporary secular university. This reconceived discipline retains its identity as a normative, prescriptive enterprise, but the norms that it constructs are fashioned within the institutional framework of the pluralistic university. So the problem of the contrast between the prescriptive theology of a religious community and the descriptive religious studies of the secular university is solved by making theology both pluralistic and normative, and by expanding the scope of religious studies departments to include

17

the discipline of normative reflection while affirming the intention
of these programs to remain secular.

The contention that theology has a justifiable position
within the study of religion can be demonstrated by setting forth the
general outline of a program of religious studies--by demarcating the
major areas of the religion curriculum, and showing the interrela-
tions among these spheres. Only then will theology be shown to have
a rightful claim to a place within the totality of religious studies.

II

The study of religion can be divided into three parts:
(1) a self-reflective, (2) a historical, and (3) a constructive part.
The self-reflective sphere concerns itself with the questions of the
nature of religion and of the methods for its investigation. The
historical portion treats the historical materials of religion (including extant theological writings) in the light of the methods established by the self-reflective mode; it is a descriptive discipline. And the constructive part, or theology as a normative discipline, is concerned with the character of correct religion.[2] The
first two parts are common in current programs of religious studies;
the third, while sometimes present implicitly, needs to be self-
consciously included in these programs.

(1) Any cognitive discipline finds it necessary to become
aware of itself, in the sense that it must inquire into both the
nature of its subject matter and the proper methods to be used in
the investigation of this subject matter. The study of religion is
no exception; it, too, is forced at one point or another to be self-
reflective. The first task of this reflection is that of establishing the nature of religion, of defining religion. Philosophers and
phenomenologists of religion who have viewed religion, for example,
as "the immediate self-consciousness of absolute dependence," as "ultimate concern," as "the element of the sacred," and as "the appre-
hension of power," have been involved in this form of self-reflection.
These definitions often involve showing the relationship of religion
to the other areas of human concern, i.e., indicating its relation to
the various cultural spheres, such as politics, economics, art, science, and philosophy. Then, after it has defined religion, reflection must establish the methods for its systematic study: it must
justify the methods to be used both in treating the historical material of religion and in constructing a normative theological position.
For example, it must determine the relative adequacy of historical,
sociological, and psychohistorical methods for understanding the
religious phenomena; it must evaluate the problem of reductionism and
the possibility of a sui generis method; and it must develop a hermeneutical theory for guiding the interpretation of the historical expressions of religion.

(2) The historical section of religious studies consists
of the treatment of the actual subject matter, the phenomena of religion which have found expression in history. The extent of the historical domain is universal. It includes the religious phenomena
from all periods of chronological history--the archaic, the

traditional, the medieval, the modern, and the contemporary; it encompasses phenomena from all cultural areas of the world, with no
preference being given to the materials of the "great" civilizations
and the "world" religions; it embraces what are usually regarded as
"cultural" phenomena, whenever they contain a religious intent; and
it encompasses all types of religious phenomena--cultic acts and
sacred spaces, as well as mythical and theological formulations. And
all of these phenomena are subject to uniform investigative principles; they are approached by the methods determined by the self-
reflective mode. This means that the historical investigator should
harbor no hidden "theological" assumptions, that his inevitable commitments should not be discernible in his work. His task is purely
descriptive. His treatment of the extra-canonical literature of the
tradition from which he receives most of his sustenance, for example,
utilizes the same methods as does his work on the canonical literature of this tradition; for both bodies of literature contain expressions of specific modes of being religious.

The relationship between the self-reflective and the historical parts of the study of religion is not a linear one, in the
sense that reflection would be both logically and chronologically
prior to research into the phenomena. The relation is, rather, one
of dialectical interdependence. This mutual dependence is present,
first of all, in the relationship between the task of defining the
nature of religion and that of investigating the historical material
of religion. On the one hand, the historical part is obviously dependent upon the self-reflective one, for it is impossible to investigate the phenomena of religion unless one knows what religion is
beforehand, unless religion has already been defined. And there is a
less obvious dependence in the other direction: religion cannot be
defined apart from an acquaintance with the material of religion.
This does not mean that religion is defined by the abstractive pro-
cedure--that is, that one arrives at the "essence" of religion by
discerning what all the instances of religion have in common. Close
scrutiny reveals that this procedure is circular, since it presupposes an understanding of religion to begin with; for in knowing what
is going to count as an instance of religion, it already knows what
religion is. This circle suggests that the determination of the
nature of religion is not a matter of discovery, but is rather one
of postulation: to offer a definition of religion is to give a rule
for the consistent use of the term "religion." However, we cannot
conclude from this that postulation is a wholly arbitrary matter.
The act of postulating is subject to the stricture that a definition
of religion must not diverge so far from the ordinary usages of the
term "religion" that confusion results. But the conventional uses
presuppose an acquaintance with the phenomena of religion, so that
definition is indeed dependent on the historical material.[3]--Then, in
the second place, there is also a dialectical dependence between the
determination of method and the historical part. Just as it is not
possible to deal with the material without a refined methodology, so
it is impossible to construct this method apart from a knowledge of
the phenomena, because the method to be employed must be appropriate
to the subject matter it has been chosen to investigate.

(3) While the historical portion of religious studies deals
with given phenomena, and is descriptive, the constructive part is a

creative discipline, and is prescriptive--that is to say, it creates
norms. For example, if religion is defined by the self-reflective
section as belief in supernatural power, and the history of religion
exhibits a series of types of this belief--belief in one God, or in
two antithetical ones, or in many, or in none--, the theologian may
erect as normative the belief in but one God; or if religion is defined as salvation, and the history of religion describes the variety
of views of salvation which have appeared--for example, salvation
from the painful world of matter, from social chaos, from sin, or
from absurdity--, the theologian may create as normative a mode of
salvation from a sin which leads to social chaos. Constructive theology, then, is that area of the study of religion in which the question of truth is asked and answered. But the truth which theology
seeks and establishes is an existential truth of conviction. For in
religion, as in other areas of the humanities, truth is established
neither deductively nor in an inductive way: pure reason cannot determine how one ought to be, religiously speaking, nor can one discover how to be solely by empirical investigation. This does not
mean that theology is not a cognitive discipline. It is; but its
discipline takes the form of investigating the decision which the
theologian has made about religious truth--that is, of working through
the implications of just this wager, as opposed to other possible
ones. So every theology is based upon a creative decision; this decision is normative, or true, for the theologian; and the work of
the theologian consists in the systematic investigation of this wager
or decision. Basic theological arguments are neither lost nor won.
They continue indefinitely, and the point at issue is always the
fundamental decision behind the entire edifice.

The relationship of constructive work to both the self-
reflective and the historical modes is one of linear dependence, for
constructive theology is determined by both of the preceding elements
of the total curriculum without exerting a counter influence of its
own. This does not mean, however, that the theological area of religious studies is dispensable. Theology is dependent upon the prior
work of self-reflection, both indirectly, through the mediating historical element, and in several direct ways. The construction of a
religious norm is obviously dependent on the definition of the essence of religion, since the norm is but a more exact specification
of the general essence. And the reflective part of the study of
religion, by establishing the methods for the other two parts, naturally determines the theological procedure.

The relationship between historical study and theology is
most important for the understanding of the position of the theological discipline, and thus requires a more extended discussion. The
fundamental relation between these two parts of the study of religion
can be described in two statements. First of all: the basic function of the history of religion is to provide sources for the constructive work of theology. For the theologian can only construct
his normative system with the historical panorama in view. And second, a corollary statement: the constructive discipline is the goal
of the historical one--indeed, it is the goal of the entire study of
religion. This is not to say that theology in any way interferes
with the integrity of historical work. And it is not to deny that
the history of religion can be pursued for its own sake. It is to

affirm, however, that the central import of the historical element
appears only when this element is seen as providing sources for the
creative work of theology.

These propositions leave several questions in their wake.
Which historical materials constitute the sources for theology? Why
is the history of religion (including the history of the religious
element in culture) significant for theological work? Indeed, why
are historical sources necessary at all for the constructive enterprise? And exactly how does theology utilize the sources which the
historical element presents to it? The answers to these questions
will clarify the nature of this reconceived theology.

The range of sources which the historical discipline presents to the constructive one is limited only by the boundaries of
the historical discipline itself--that is, only by the boundaries of
human history. Ideally, of course, the history of religion studies
every extant expression of religion that it can locate. And the
historian of religion presents all of these expressions to the theologian for his evaluation. This means that, in principle, all of the
historical phenomena of religion can function as sources for theology.
True to his pluralistic framework, the university theologian has
access to all traditions, and is not limited to any one of them. It
may be that a theologian finds one tradition, or even one narrow area
within a tradition, to be more congenial to his religious exigency
than other traditions or areas; but he makes no a priori commitment
to limit himself to anything less than the universal scope of the
general history of religion. The theological enterprise which exists
within a secular context, then, is a multi-tradition discipline, and
its practitioners intentionally immerse themselves in a variety of
historical sources.

But the history of religion includes many types of religious phenomena--myths, rituals, symbols, etc., as well as theological systems. Can all of these types of historical material be
sources for constructive work, or are theological systems alone candidates for scrutiny by normative theology? In order to answer this
question, it is necessary to distinguish between explicit and implicit theologies--a distinction which, though not absolute, is nevertheless useful. Now, explicit theologies are those which are consciously scientific in the sense that they are intentionally cognitive and are thus already systematic. Implicit theologies, on the
other hand, are those which are of a naive and unconscious sort, but
which implicitly contain and express a theological perception of
religious truth. All types of religious phenomena, then, are expressions of a religious stance, and those expressions which are implicitly theological are so because they have not yet been translated
into a structured theological idiom. So in principle, all materials
of the history of religion, from Paul Tillich's utterly explicit
Systematic Theology to an implicit Polynesian creation myth, are
sources for theological construction. Implicit theologies, though,
in order to be available to the theologian for constructive work,
must be translated into theological terms: for example, myths must
be demythologized, and the religious significance of cultural
materials must be discovered and cast into the corresponding theological language.[4]

The historical material of religion is both significant and necessary for constructive theology. It is significant, because all of the various theological positions, explicit or implicit, that mankind has assumed throughout the course of history represent possibilities for the theologian's own position. That is, every religious stance expressed in a historical formulation represents a permanent possibility for subsequent stances, for each standpoint mankind has assumed in history is capable of being indefinitely repeated. Indeed, each standpoint calls for such repetition, just by virtue of its implicit claim to be true. It is not a question, however, of repeating the historical conditions (e.g., the language, the culture) of the initial stance. A distinction must be made within the historical material between that which is permanently possible in it and that which is temporal and historical, between the essential and the accidental, between that which is repeatable and that which cannot be repeated. What is repeatable is not the form of the expression, which is historically relative and accidental; what can be repeated is, rather, that which is expressed, the basic and ideal religious stance which has come to temporal expression within the specific material. But to say that the totality of the contents of historical expressions represent repeatable possibilities for the theologian is not to say that he cannot transcend the possibilities presented to him by his sources; he is not necessarily doomed to a mere repetition, for the development of a novel position is itself always a possibility. But even if the theologian is successful in expressing a novel posture in the world of religion, this stance is determined, if only negatively, by his sources.

If the history of religion is significant for theology because it presents permanent possibilities for a creative decision, it is necessary for several reasons. First of all, the implicit claims to truth of a multitude of historical standpoints impinge upon the theologian, calling forth his response in the form of a synthetic statement of his own. More importantly, the theologian cannot construct a normative system within a historical vacuum: he requires the material of history in order to elicit his own judgments. For constructive work presupposes a knowledge of various possibilities for construction, and possibilities are known, not a priori, but through an encounter with historical phenomena. It is the encounter with other standpoints which shapes and defines the stance of the theologian. The old question, "How do I know what I think until I see what I say?" can be altered slightly to make the point: how do I know what I think until I see how I react?

Because of the indefinite number of sources presented to him by the history of religion, the theologian faces the problem of selection. He may be tempted to allow either his own historical interests and specialties, or his own situation within a religious or cultural tradition, to act, consciously or unconsciously, as his principle of selection. But in view of the statement that sources function as such because they represent possibilities for the theologian's own constructive position, these principles are obviously inadequate. The principle of selection should instead be that of variety. In other words, the theologian's selection should be made to cover the widest possible assortment of theological positions

expressed in the course of history. Variety, of course, is by no
means simply a matter of chronological and geographical diversity;
it is also, and particularly, a matter of the diversity of theological possibilities.

But once the selection is made according to the principle
of variety, how does theology utilize its wealth of chosen sources?
It is clear that   the theologian cannot positively appropriate
all of the possibilities represented by his sources--this would not
at all be possible, since some of these sources express positions
which are mutually exclusive. Theology utilizes the sources by means
of a critique, or evaluation, of them. This evaluation cannot be in
the light of an actually existent position which is regarded as absolutely valid, for if this were the case, theology would find these
sources superfluous to begin with. Rather, the evaluation must be
in the light of the other sources. This means that evaluation is
ultimately a matter of comparison, so that the criteria for judgment
always arise in the very process of comparing. And these criteria
are not "given"; they are created by the theologian in an act of
decision. The alternatives for decision are present in the sources
themselves--but in the sources as they are arranged for the act of
decision by the comparative study of the materials.[5] After the alternatives have been established, the theologian makes a decision,
which may be either synthetic or exclusive, and which is cast into
the form of a constructive system.

III

Theology, as a normative and pluralistic discipline, has a
legitimate and necessary place within the religious studies program.
Its legitimacy is shown by the fact that it occupies a logical position in the structure of the curriculum I have described. Its neces-
ity is demonstrated by the fact that the self-reflective and historical elements of the study of religion are incomplete until they are
complemented by the constructive mode. For the creation of norms is
the final goal of religious studies. This is to say that the real
impetus behind the investigation of religion is not a mere intellectual or aesthetic curiosity, but is a desire for existential truth.
It might be said that the primary purpose of the tasks of establishing the nature and methods of religion is to aid and guide historical investigation, and that the goal of historical research is not
simply to discover what was expressed, but through this discovery to
help the contemporary decide what should be expressed today.

According to the common conception, theology exists within
and in the interests of a single tradition; but in my reconception of
it, theology exists in a pluralistic framework and is accordingly
trans-traditional. Now, in the eyes of the former, the latter notion
of theology might be regarded as misguided because it neglects the
important consideration that we only stand within one tradition, to
which we are native and which is familiar to us, and that other
traditions are too strange to us to be sources for our constructive
thought.

Several replies can be made to this natural objection.

First of all, the contention that "other" traditons are foreign to us but that our own is not, must be disputed. There is in fact a historical distance existing between us and every religious expression of history, so that there is no difference in principle, only a difference in degree, between an expression from our own tradition and one from another. Indeed, one of the enduring contributions of biblical studies in this century has been the discovery of the strangeness of the thought-forms of the biblical literature of the "western" traditions to us. So if it is a matter of relative strangeness, there is no reason to conclude that the material of other traditions ought to be excluded from constructive consideration by the theologian. Then, the objection presupposes a conception of religious traditions as static, unvarying entities with an identifiable essence. But is it not rather the case that traditions are fluid realities continually in a state of shifting flux, in accordance with the changes of cultural patterns? Traditions might be conceived of as streams flowing into other traditions, continually forming new ones. The fabric of our cultural and religious life, then, is composed of a multiplicity of traditions intersecting in our existence. This was true of Philo Judaeus, who was heir to the traditions of Platonism, Stoicism, and Judaism; it was true of Augustine, who synthesized a philosophical and an ecclesiastical tradition; and it is true of us, who are in a position to amalgamate insights from Freud, Marx, and the dominant religious tradition. So, though it may be the case that we are inevitably located within one tradition, this one stream is continually changing and expanding, always open for an influx from other tributaries. And everything within the giant stream of the human tradition confronts us with a permanent possibility for our own religious position.

The inevitable question of the relationship between the theology of a religious studies program and that of the religious community cannot be discussed here at any length, for it involves the larger question of the relation between religious communions and the general society. But it should be clear that the university theologian can be, though he need not be, a member of a religious group; thus his constructive position may legitimately show clear signs of a special indebtedness to the sources native to that communion. The difference between his work as a theologian within a secular framework and the work he would have done in an ecclesiastical context, though, is clear: as a university theologian, he does not artificially and in principle limit himself to one set of sources; but as a seminary theologian, his work would enjoy a communal effectiveness by virtue of the fact that it would represent a degree of consensus within his religious community.[6] For the strength of university theology is that its openness to the multiplicity of available sources makes its products richer than are those of the "church" form of theology. But the strength of ecclesiastical theology is that its judgments, being communal, are more effective than are the formulations of the secular theologian, who thinks and speaks only as an individual among individuals.

---

[1]The term "theology" can have both a special and a general meaning; it can refer to specifically Christian theology, and it can denote, by extension, the doctrinal inquiry present in all religious

traditions. Here the word is used only in the latter, more general
sense. See Ninian Smart, Secular Education and the Logic of Religion (London: Faber and Faber, 1968), p. 10.

[2]This brief statement, and the explication of it which
follows, should be construed in the most formal of ways: this "map"
of the terrain occupied by religious studies neither presupposes nor
yields any positions on what religion is, on the correct methods for
its investigation, on the nature of the historical materials, or on
what constitutes normative religion. It is intended only as a framework within which significant discussion (i.e., material agreement
and disagreement) can occur.

[3]For two discussions of the problem of the definition of
religion, see: Paul Tillich, Religionsphilosophie, in Gesammelte
Werke, ed. Renate Albrecht, Band 1: Fruehe Hauptwerke (Stuttgart:
Evangelisches Verlagswerk, 1959), pp. 304-317; and Robert D. Baird,
Category Formation and the History of Religions (The Hague: Mouton),
pp. 1-16.

[4]Models of this process of translation include Rudolf Bult-
mann's work of demythologizing the mythological language of the New
Testament, Mircea Eliade's interpretation of archaic myths, symbols,
and rituals, and Paul Tillich's treatment of the religious substance
of cultural forms.

[5]The comparative study of religion, then, is not a part
of historical studies but is a sub-discipline of theology. Though
it contains descriptive elements, it stands in the service of theology proper. Comparison is, of course, a matter of exhibiting both
similarities and differences: it is the ultimate similarities of
religious phenomena which make them religious; it is the differences
which make the theological decision necessary.

[6]See Paul Tillich, Das System der Wissenschaften nach Gegen-
staenden und Methoden, in Gesammelte Werke, Band 1, p. 261: "Effective legal (and religious) conviction is . . . never the theoretical
conviction of an individual, but is rather the practical conviction
of a community."

THE HOME TEAM

Denise L. Carmody
The Pennsylvania State University

This paper reports on the experiences of a wife-husband team in undergraduate teaching, and then speculates on their implications. After describing the courses taught, it begins the speculation by analyzing student enthusiasm and teacher stimulation, both of which have seemed significantly high. The final sections of the paper ruminate on the implications for religious studies and theology that such team-teaching suggests.

Courses Taught

The courses furnishing our experience are "Introduction to Religion," "The Religious Mind," and "Contemporary Self-Discovery." "Introduction to Religion" is a first level course averaging about 50 students per section. Explicitly, it is a "service course" for the university. That is, its role is to provide a general introduction to religion, open to anyone interested: liberal arts student, engineer, physical education major, etc. Hence, the students it attracts cover the spectrum: the merely curious, the potential major, the "need-something-outside-my-field-to-fulfill-a-requirement" types.

Initially we each taught the course alone, using short novels (e.g., Wiesel's NIGHT, Kane's AMBIGUOUS ADVENTURE, Moore's THE LONELY PASSION OF JUDITH HEARNE), scriptures (e.g., THE HEART SUTRA, THE TAO-TE-CHING, THE GOSPEL ACCORDING TO JOHN), and expository works (e.g., Kapleau's THE THREE PILLARS OF ZEN, Berger's A RUMOR OF ANGELS, Alexander's THE WORLD'S RIM). Joachim Wach's THE COMPARATIVE STUDY OF RELIGION provided a theoretic framework. Each of us felt the course was successful, but not completely so. The main difficulty was a feeling of "So what?" in ourselves and in the students. The scope of the course -- primitive religion, Hinduism, Buddhism, Taosim, Confucianism, Judaism, Christianity, Islam in ten weeks -- necessitates a survey approach. Surveys often become travelogues: fleeting glimpses, minimal experience, no little confusion. And, given the diverse audience, the probability of avoiding the pitfalls of the survey course, by organizing a common attack or building a profile of homo religiosus, seemed low. Lectures providing background were well-received; discussions stimulating personal integration were discouragingly rare.

What "Introduction to Religion" sought from the team, then, was a catalyst for integrating the materials of a world-religious survey into patterns personally coherent and significant for the general student. To our gratification, the sought was found. It appears to have been found mainly because with two teachers one was free to specialize in specification, application, contemporary parallels. The format we used was half-hour expository lecture, ten minute "reaction" by the second teacher, and then open discussion (all of which assumed prior reading of specific textual materials). From week to week, we swapped the roles of lecturer and reactor.

27

Somehow, the reaction bridged lecture and discussion in a way that neither of us had been able to achieve alone. Whether this came from the reactor's freedom to boil the lecture down, watch the students for areas of non-comprehension, or make personal appropriations is not clear. Maybe just having the lecturer engaged or challenged or overtly interpreted "equalized" him or her down from the podium to the hoi polloi. At any rate, the discussions were far more engaging than they had been in the solo "Introductions."

"The Religious Mind" was an upper division seminar with an enrollment of fourteen. Of the fourteen, nine were seniors, four juniors, one a sophomore. The academic spectrum was narrow. Nearly all were straight "A" students. Their majors were all within the College of Liberal Arts: five in religious studies, four in humanities, three in psychology, one each in philosophy and advertising. We described the goal of the course as "an increased awareness of the differentiations requisite for a properly contemporary, sophisticated view of religious consciousness." The means we listed as intense study -- reading and common analysis -- of two recent books on the religious mind. The books -- Bernard Lonergan's METHOD IN THEOLOGY and John Bowker's THE SENSE OF GOD -- offer detailed analyses of religious intentionality, in order to ground theology and investigate how the sense of God arises in human consciousness. Lonergan marries neo-Thomist cognitional theory to contemporary appreciation of symbolism and historicity; Bowker looks through the lenses of such diverse disciplines as anthropology, phenomenology, psychology, systems analysis, and structuralism. The seminar met one evening a week for three hours.

Our reasons in divising this course were several. One, we had each read the books and found them highly provocative. Two, we had each taught students who not only were capable of quality work but also had indicated interest in a course like this. Three, we wanted to test the validity of our initial evaluation of team-teaching in a more selective situation. The results of "The Religious Mind" have both nuanced and confirmed our first verdicts on team-teaching. Their confirmation lies in the students' enthusiasm and hard work which were even more impressive than "Introduction to Religion's" students', since the work was more demanding. For the first time, we heard students speak of re-reading an assignment, and one even reported Lonergan's positive dominance of his dreams. The nuance stems from the different form of teaching in "The Religious Mind." Almost entirely, it was run as a discussion-seminar. This meant that our "team" interacted or coordinated less formally, more subtly, than in "Introduction's" lecture-response format. Spontaneously, more of our personal differences, inextricably tied to sexual differences (whether from roles or glands), came through. The female students, especially, seemed to appreciate seeing a woman treated as an "equal:" being independent, winning and losing skirmishes, correcting and being corrected. More than in "Introduction," they seemed to be identifying with a viable role model. So, in general, the less formal format increased our personal exposure and correspondingly drew students into more personal engagements with issues than seems normally to occur.

As I write, "Contemporary Religious Self-Discovery" has not yet been taught. We will teach it during the summer quarter, 1975. However, I include it in the report because it is designed to focus still more directly on what we have learned in our team-teaching, and because it will have been done by the time we meet to discuss this paper.

The course again is upper division, with an enrollment probably between 10-15. The summer student population has an older segment: school teachers and others completing degree requirements or seeking professional advancement by taking additional courses. So, we are planning the course with an eye toward the possibility that some of the students will have broad "extracurricular" experience.

The books we will be reading together are Carlos Castenenda's TALES OF POWER, Robert Pirsig's ZEN AND THE ART OF MOTORCYCLE MAINTENANCE, and Doris Lessing's THE GOLDEN NOTEBOOK. The title of the course sets the goal: a study of three modern autobiographies depicting three distinctive efforts to achieve "religious" self-discovery. Castenenda becomes an apprentice to a Yaqui wise man. Pirsig travels within himself and his society as he cycles from Minnesota to the West Coast with his small son. Lessing explores the psyche of the "liberated" woman fettered by self-doubt and societal hypocrisy. For each, the search is a drive for wholeness, human fulfillment, salvation from the alienations that sunder the human spirit. Thus, each search is a religious quest.

Because one of the books is explicitly feminist, we expect that the dual focus of our team will be heightened. Because all of the books orchestrate the themes of personal journeying, we hope that they will bring making life, sharing life, to the fore. Self-discovery is centrally finding one's path into mystery, one's compact with chiaroscuro. When it can be shared, it is immensely enriched and eased -- as every Sangha and profound friendship intuits. Perhaps most marriages, or even most "meetings" of hearts disposed to seek, also intuit this. At any rate, we hope to track loves like eros, philia, agape, in the course of studying three contemporary hunters of enlightenment and wholeness.

Student Enthusiasm

As I reflect on the pedagogical implications of our team-teaching, I must rank student enthusiasm as both a major result and a decisive criterion. It is what generates an atmosphere where teaching-learning-sharing is exciting and almost inevitable. It is what proves to us and to our students that the venture is worthwhile. The kind of enthusiasm we have seen team-teaching create is marked by an eagerness to take part in discussions, a tendency to linger after class or to drop in during office hours to continue a line of argument, a willingness to concretize insights by examples from personal experience. In our eyes, this is evidence that growth is occurring.

For, the material involved is never "easy." Lonergan, Bowker, Lessing cannot be understood on one reading. Here, again, students' response is enlightening: they find themselves working harder than they normally do -- and, for the first half of the course, feeling they are understanding less than they normally do. But, since they see it as a communal enterprise -- and since we show that we too are struggling for deeper understanding -- initial discouragement acts more as a catalyst than a depressant. Something in the team struggle of the teachers makes the student strugglers a team.

Gradually, the students begin to sense the integrity of a text. They find analogies in their own experience; they see implications for areas outside the material's immediate domain. In sharing these, they spur the rest of us to appropriate what we are reading. Our focus is either explicitly or at least implicitly on religious conscious-ness -- in "Introduction," to appreciate the religions of the world by trying to probe the ways they reflect the human quest for response to the Ultimate; in "The Religious Mind" and "Contemporary Self-Discovery," to bear directly on religious intentionality and the self's struggle for wisdom. In each course, we aim to help the students per-ceive themselves as well as the data: to attend to the workings of their religious con-sciousness as well as to "religious consciousness" in general, or in their texts.

For example, in a conversation outside class recently, a student remarked that he had been critical of Lonergan's theories on cognition. He found the material dif-ficult and he wasn't sure it was all that valid. Then, he said with a smile, he found him-self working through a problem according to Lonergan's method. Further, he realized that this is the way his mind regularly operates. Thus, he validated the theory in his own consciousness. His quiet amusement belied a feeling of genuine achievement -- a satisfaction too seldom felt in academia.

Another contributor to student enthusiasm is implied in the title of this paper: "The Home Team." Where the number of students and the size of one's living-room allow, the palpable value of meeting at home makes it worth considering seriously. (Later I will explore another dimension of this under theological implications.) Students appreciate that this kind of gesture is beyond the scope of duty. They sense it means more work -- many of them live off-campus and realize that guests call for some pre-planning. Many are dorm-dwellers who doubly appreciate a home atmosphere. All, at our large institution, say invitations to a professor's home are rare. So, there is a milieu of appreciation, friendliness, and openness in the home situation that subtly adds to students' responsiveness. Little of this may be verbalized, but it seems beyond dis-pute.

Because we live three miles from campus and public transportation is meager, it is not possible for us to meet at home regularly. However, we arrange for several spaced sessions at home. Perhaps this is the better route to take: it achieves the atmosphere we desire, yet avoids the draw-backs routine might produce. Typically, the most apparent breakthrough occurs during the first home session. The setting seems to stimulate new levels of communication: there is gentle teasing when someone presents an objection; support for another's position is also more vocal. During the coffee/milk/Fresca break, the discussion continues in small groups on the balcony, in the kitchen, and among those lotused on the living-room floor. In our experience, this tangible sense of community percolates for the rest of the course. With the sexual role-modeling mentioned above, it seems an important stimulus to personal involvement in the course work, and so to better quality and profit.

Teacher Stimulation

This second pedagogical yield has had its impact even in the courses we teach alone. Because we do share one course a year, we have learned to work very closely in a course's planning and execution. In "Introduction," where, as noted, large enrollment necessitates a more structured approach, we alternated responsibility for lecture and discussion, on a weekly basis. Students quickly felt free to offer their opinions after seeing it done first by one of us. Similarly, we were each able to fill in any oversights the other missed in her or his presentation. "The Religious Mind" and "Contemporary Self-Discovery" follow a modified version of the above. Prime responsibility falls on one; commentator or stimulator responsibility falls on the other. This means that one prepares with a mind toward clarification and exposition, the other with a mind toward implications, exemplifications, significance. So while we both have preparation, the time it takes varies each week, giving one more "free" time to write, read, do research. A plus in team-teaching, then, is the reduction of time spent in class preparation. Obviously, this is not the chief advantage, and team-teaching is not efficient for a department. In fact, each time we do it one of us is working for free -- or for the other's slightly greater freedom.

For us, the major advantage has been the experience itself. We enjoy teaching together. We learn from one another's insights; we stimulate one another to be more precise, nuanced, profound even! As well, we have a basis from which to explore new techniques that might improve all our courses, because we are regularly criticizing one another's performance. Since we work together planning the course, from calendar to exam questions, we know one another as "teachers" much better. Thus, we can be much more detailed in our advice than we could be before we taught together. In addition, teaching together has established a channel for regular sharing of any pedagogical finds or problems. For instance, a new way to encourage discussion discovered by one will very likely be tried in our joint-venture or adopted by the other in her or his solo teaching. Or a film that one finds useful, the back of the other's head will file. Further, even in those areas where our interests differ, there is more overlap than we once supposed. So John's interest in primitive religion can touch mine in women's studies: e.g., the majority of Japanese shamans have been women. We are now quicker to alert one another to material we find "in the other's fields"; and there is more natural cause to be reading and discussing the same books and articles, even if for different ends. Such discussions not only supply a fuller context for all our reading, they also often prompt complementary insights, because of our different horizons.

To develop the implications of the stimulus and complementarity I have been describing, let me extend my ruminations into three different subsections of undergraduate teaching: 1) scholarly interpretation, 2) use of disparate talents and interests, and 3) role-modeling. The first, scholarly interpretation, is something first pointed out to us by our students. They were quick to see how sexual differences or conditioning prompt different interpretations of data. While trying to avoid stereotypic mentalities, we still find that we sometimes zero in on material from opposite sides. Probing our "differences" sometimes reveals interesting variations. For instance, to me "God" conjures up love, acceptance, nearness. For John, "God" more readily connotes mystery, otherness. It seems good for students to witness such legitimate diversity, and it may exemplify the contribution to God's trans-sexist naming that theologies could take from wife-husband teams.

Further, because the major portion of the texts we use are male-authored, their perspective often is deficient, compared to our duality. Since we try to make the atmosphere of our discussions open, the pointing out of such deficiency or imbalance is subject to clarification and nuance. Thus, the deficiency is genuinely instructive and the corrective usually avoids polemic. Lonergan's METHOD IN THEOLOGY became an example of this. His illustrations are frequently sexual stereotypes, but far more telling is the awkwardness with which he speaks of human love and interpersonal relationships. His "mates" have the spark and warmth of terms in an algebraic equation. Our aim, I hope, is not to denigrate Lonergan's precision but rather to save it from rationalism by finding more wholistic expressions. And our efforts to do this seem to free the students to offer the nuances they feel are needed. (It is easy to forget that students also have experiences, perspectives, horizons which offer legitimate correctives to text and teacher alike. The greater openness fostered by the team has lessened our forgetting).

Second, the use of disparate talents and interests is an integral part of team-teaching's rationale, and one of its most instructive facets. While our professional training shares similarities, our teaching talents are rather different. I can easily reproduce factual details in their chronological or causal sequence with considerable accuracy, supplying analogies to point up their relevance. John's forte is less extensive, more intensive. He can pinpoint the heart of the matter and lay out its implications. Here again we find a natural collusion between talent and economy: more time to do what we do best. Though we swap roles, I am probably the more natural expositor, John the more natural reactor. However, we have found that the specific "talent" of one can be more readily assimilated by the other when it is encountered regularly, cooperatively, first-hand. In fact, we learn, almost by osmosis, techniques which broaden our individual competencies.

The disparity of our interests has the same implications: it exposes us to a wider span of experiences and tends to make research time more judiciously spent. There is an additional asset, too. The complementarity of our interests generates a richer context than either has alone. This is hard to illustrate because it is more qualitative than quantitative. Perhaps it is the result of enthusiasms-shared, mutual stimulation, whatever. But the fact is one plus one yields more than two. By working together, we have a sharper heuristic, a richer curiosity alone.

Role-modeling, the third implication, is an area where the results have been more impressive than we anticipated. The paucity of women professors is one reason; the virtual non-existence of wife-husband combinations is another. Both men and women students benefit more than we expected from the interaction of a team like ours. That they see something novel and important seems clear. What they see is behind their eye-balls, but we hope it is neither Tarzan-Jane nor Maggie-Jiggs. We hope it is the cooperation of equals. Such cooperation seems to be contagious. One noticeable effect in class is that the comments of both sexes are taken equally seriously -- supported or challenged without the games often found in mixed groups. Because of sexual bias in university life, the women students' reactions are more apparent or dramatic, as I mentioned earlier. Initially, most are passive. Rather quickly, however, sensing our sympathy, they become assertive, with even a tinge of "So, there." By mid-quarter, the atmosphere has relaxed: the confidence of the women has grown enough to round out sharp edges.

The metamorphosis of the men is more subtle. Initially, they are the ones who speak out. Then, as the women become more assertive, the men become more wary. Most seem bewildered. Some appear resentful. Only a few are unaffected. Gradually,

33

the tensions ease and sexual differences count for less than individual differences.
Neither John nor I have been able to duplicate this liberation alone.

Finally, our team naturally doubles opportunities for meeting students' very
varied needs. This we see most clearly in the "pattern" students follow in seeking either
John or me for outside help or further discussion. There is no pattern. Thus far, students seem to make their choices between us in terms of what they perceive as our competence to deal with their particular problem. There has been no division along sexual
lines, nor even any clear-cut identification with one of us. Students appear willing,
eager to "use" both of us according to their needs. In fact, in several instances, where
a student had had more contact with one of us during the first three weeks of a course,
he or she deliberately sought out the other, saying, "I haven't had much chance to talk
with you" or "I've been wondering how you feel about...." Thus, we feel the role-
modeling effected by a male-female team is especially suited for promoting students'
individual development by providing realistic examples of the complementarity (rather
than the polarity) of sexual differences.

Generally, then, we have found team-teaching stimulating because it en-
hances each member's work, and serves students' needs, in ways that solo courses
have not.

Religious Studies Implications

Just as there seem to be pedagogical implications in the team experience,
so too there seem to be implications for religious studies. By religious studies I mean
the discipline which attempts to understand religion and religions without reliance on
or promotion of their faiths. Admittedly, this is a rough, perhaps impossible, description. I fashion it here neither prescriptively nor definitionally -- only indicatively.
The larger question of Religious Studies vis-a-vis Theology deserves fuller treatment
in another time and place. My present concern is both narrower and, I think, more
pressing: how can we help our students gain insight into the meaning of religion and
into specific religions, while they stand outside most religions' doctrinal and cultic
experience of faith? How can we help them to objective knowledge?

One method is to clarify the meaning of objectivity and show how a person
achieves it. Here I find the cognitional theory of Bernard Lonergan instructive.[1] For
Lonergan, objectivity is the fruit of authentic subjectivity. Unpacked, this assertion
yields a line of reasoning like the following. Knowing is constituted by three basic
operations: experiencing, understanding, and judging. Each operation is part to a
whole. For instance, when we experience something new, we try to understand it.
Once understanding occurs, further questions arise: is this understanding correct?
Is it so? Only when these further questions are answered can we make the judgment:
this is so, or it is not so. And, only when we can thus affirm or deny is there full
human knowledge.

Knowledge, then, is the cumulative result of personal experience, understanding, and judgment. They key word here is personal. Unlike a computer, a person
is free. She or he is capable of raising the questions which catalyze the movement from
experience, through understanding, to judgment. "Capable of" is not "bound to." One

can refuse to raise further questions, or be so blinded by self-interest that understanding is blocked or judgment warped. For instance, most smokers are aware of the surgeon general's data and conclusions. They have experience of hacking and information on its import. Their understanding may even have been tutored by seeing pictures of tar-blackened lungs, or having had associates who died from lung cancer. And surely others have told them that their fumes are unwelcome. Yet, their judgment is not an automatic, decisive "no cigarettes for me ever again." Why? Because a judgment is a personal stand, something taken only when one determines that the evidence at hand is sufficient and convincing. Thus the final arbiter is the person judging. Hence, clarity about personal biases, self-interest, moods is essential if one's judgment is to be mature, objective, realistic. Objectivity demands profound, authentic subjectivity. The ancient oracle speaks today: "Know thyself."

So "objectivity" -- that vaunted ideal of religious studies' adolescence -- will have to be personal and cumulative in its maturity.[2] As Lonergan explains, the data of experience have the objectivity of given facts; one's understanding of the data has a normative objectivity; one's judgment has an absolute (though not infallible) objectivity: "As far as I can determine, this is so."[3] Since Kierkegaard praised repetition (as well as subjectivity), I'll say it again: objectivity is the fruit of authentic subjectivity. It is achieved not by an empty-headed staring at brute facts, nor by their detached in-gesting, nor by some automatic judgmental printout. Human knowing is an integrated personal activity demanding authenticity: attentive experience, intelligent understanding, rational judgment.[4]

With a cognitional theory like this in hand, there are definite tools one can offer students for their work of coming to know themselves -- coming to appropriate their mental structures so that they can enflesh reasonableness and enact love. For example, most of our students find Buddhism new and foreign. Its emphasis on stilling desires, emptiness, anatta can be a genuine challenge to understanding. Here the need is for constant clarification, analogous examples from their own experience, shared effort to penetrate the terms and, as far as possible, appropriate the experience. For our part, as teachers, the need is both to help them do this and to show them why doing this -- rather than memorizing Sanskrit terms -- is the key to understanding. But after they have achieved some understanding, they should be led to judgment: is this true? Too many students are ready to answer this question before the course has begun. The fundamentalists know Buddhism is a false religion. The anti-establishments know it is true, or truer than any western religion could be. Saddest of all, a large group couldn't care or judge less. To them Buddhism is an indifferent exactment for which they will receive three credits. Of such is the kingdom no teacher can rule.

In helping students form a judgment, it is important to distinguish what is being judged. Surely, not the existence of Buddhism, nor its salvific value for millions of followers. Both are historical facts. The area for significant judgment is rather the adequacy of Buddhism's answer to humanity's efforts to find a "way through" its most intransigent limitations: suffering, evil, death.[5] A judgment here, however tentative, is what transforms a religious studies "course" into a personal problem. If I judge Buddhism an adequate answer to ultimate questions, what do I count as evidence? If I judge it inadequate, where do I see it failing? Further, what would I judge to be a more adequate answer? and why? These are the kinds of questions that force teachers

and students alike to confront values, biases, aspirations -- to confront the stuff of
their own lives.

Thus, students aided in their efforts to make reasonable judgments about
religion and the religions can begin to fashion or appropriate their own ultimate values.
Obviously, team-teaching is not the only means to this end. Nevertheless, it does have
certain advantages. Honoring the differences in viewpoints caused by sexual conditioning seems to sharpen ability to articulate self-understanding. Somehow it is easier
for two to spell out the struggle to understand data and reach value judgments, if they
have resolved conflicts from these processes within their own relationship. So, for
instance, questions of "adequacy" can be more thoroughly probed when both male and
female needs are laid out. Further, sexual differences when they are not burked, can
yield to human differences, human needs, and the pursuit of judgment can become more
wholistic. Lastly, sharing our struggles to experience, understand, and judge another
religion opens the possibility of learning from this religion. And if we are learning, we
are neither defaming nor proselytizing.

Our team's implications for religious studies, then, flow from the nuance
and consistencies that male-female duality of focus gives to transcendental method.[6] It
is not simply that our team explains yin-yang or wu-wei better than either of us would
alone. It is not just that I know THE LADY WAS A BISHOP and John knows the samurai's
Bushido Code. Rather, it is that our relationship has highlighted the delicacy of wisdom,
the viciousness of positivism, the androgyny of healthy illative sense. Thereby, we hope,
the people who try to penetrate the compound of their ultimate limitations as Muslims, Hin-
dus, Christians, Jews, whatever may receive a better shake. Together, we remember
better the dangers of hypostasis, the fallacies of misplaced concreteness. This is hum-
bling, but blessedly so. People who have shared deep hopes and fears, puzzled together over sins like racism and sexism, should be, paradoxically, both more impatient
on the need to face the Mystery and less "judgmental" about others' facings or fugues.
Since we find no excess of esprit de finesse in religious studies, we think that a team's
greater sensitivity has gifts for the field.

Theological Implications

Let theology be reflection on the significance and value of a religion in a
culture.[7] Using this definition, several theological implications of our team-teaching
come to mind. First, what we are about is precisely reflecting, weighing, considering
what religion means, intends, signifies within a given culture. Yet this is little more
than what we said in the last section on religious studies. It grows theological only
when it deals with "my God," "my ultimate," "my culture."

So, second, let us develop "religion" in this personal direction. Religion
is being rational and loving without restriction. It is the dynamic state of being-in-love
unrestrictedly. For Lonergan, experiencing, understanding, and judging are the
operations by which a person transcends herself intellectually, rationally. Such self-
transcendence is vital to personal growth. However, rational self-transcendence
should push on to decision. Most judgments raise the question, "If this is true, what
am I going to do about it?". Full, human transcendence occurs only with the answering
of such a question. It is in decision that commitment, love occur. Am I willing to do

what I judge good, fight what I judge evil? Lived religion results from decisive
commitment, existential self-transcendence. The basis of such religion is ultimate:
God, the Tao, Yahveh, Allah. Religion is being rational (experiencing, understanding,
judging) and loving (deciding) without restriction (in response to the ultimate). It is
full, wholistic -- "with all your heart and mind and soul and strength."

The implications of team reflection on such religion in our culture include
the following. First, ultimate self-transcendence through love of holy mystery power-
fully effects the liberation that human personality begs. "Salvation," "grace," "redemp-
tion" all flow from the numen's holy presence. That God has given "himself" epitomizes
Karl Rahner's theology.[8] That human nature is basically jen and yi energizes Mencian
hope.[9] For our culture, which is neither German nor Chinese, being-in-love unrestrictedly might strike the chords of a dozen oppressions. Symbolically, our team represents
the bondages of sexual oppression. Any combination of teachers, however, multiplies
the intuitions of religious needs -- and of theological words to meet them. Certainly social mixture, age mixture, mixture by economic class can serve as well as sex. The point
is any entry to the conflicted sarx that existential religion would pneumatize. As James
Cone argues, the out groups are closer to biblical experience than the in.[10] As our team
experience has shown, feminine "patience" frequently reveals ultimacy better than WASPM
control.

Second, the sharing that bonds our team is protocellular for society. Therefore, the communal dimensions of need and liberation emerge more forcefully than when
we teach alone. Sangha, ashram, ummah, synagogue, church are all numinous ideograms,
as well as houses of infirmity. Friendship and marriage are analogues of the Christian
God's union with his people. In our society, relating still seems frequently to misfire,
missing still seems regularly to abound. But "what would be left of that covenant between you and men if there were no justice here on earth, between men?".[11] Despite
his translator's sexist language, Oosterhuis' query is religiously right on. The mandate
of heaven implies human prosperity. Even when this is paradoxical, as in Euripides',
Socrates', and Jesus' play with "life" and "death," it remains true.[12] Every generation
asks signs of communion, possibilities of relating. That we at least are trying to grow
into "one flesh" seems a sign of hope to our students. That complementarity or wholeness are thought by us two, at least, not to be chimerical seems theologically significant.

It also gets results. For instance, our counseling of students from team
courses appears to be more extensive and intensive, than that of "solo" students. Their
faith lives and their love lives have been more deeply touched. What we take from this
is far less our "genius," far more the pathos of a generation with little gladness from its
elders' bones and loins.

Finally, being a team at home seems frequently to have educed our kids'
pathos. Sprawling in our apartment usually goes before confessing in our office. God
knows, we set no shingles for shriving. Only a religious studies professor resistant to
theology, however, can thoroughly disjoin teaching and healing. "Doctor" we are called.
Healers we are sometimes called, privileged to be. It is feary, trembly stuff. It's oblique,
implicit, non-direct. But when we have joy unfeigned, hospitality unfeigned, to share,
we open the way to Erikson's "generativity."[13] The home team has generated more life

than the office solos. If "the glory of God is humankind alive," this seems a theological, godly implication. Without, I hope, hubris, we're inclined to keep the team together.

References

[1] See especially Insight (New York, 1957).

[2] For personal knowledge, see Michael Polanyi, Personal Knowledge (New York, 1964).

[3] See Insight, pp. 375-384.

[4] On the religious role of authenticity, see Lonergan's Method in Theology (New York, 1972), pp. 101 ff.

[5] See John Bowker, The Sense of God (Oxford, 1973), pp. 44 ff.

[6] See Method in Theology, pp. 13 ff.

[7] See Lonergan's Philosophy of God, and Theology (Philadelphia, 1973), pp. 15, 22.

[8] See Karl Rahner, Theological Investigations, IV (Baltimore, 1966). pp. 60 ff.

[9] See Mencius, trans. W.A.C.H. Dobson (Toronto, 1963), p. 131.

[10] This is a theme of Cone's books, but it came home most vividly in a lecture he gave at Pennsylvania State University, May 5, 1975.

[11] See Huub Oosterhuis, Prayers, Poems & Songs, trans. David Smith (New York, 1970), p. 88

[12] See Eric Voegelin, "The Gospel and Culture," in D. Miller and D. Hadidian, eds., Jesus and Man's Hope, II (Pittsburgh, 1971), pp. 59-101.

[13] See Erik H. Erikson, Identity: Youth and Crisis (New York, 1968), pp. 138-139.

LIBERATION MOVEMENTS: A RELIGIOUS STUDIES UNDERGRADUATE COURSE

June O'Connor

University of California, Riverside

The course I am about to describe is, in fact, several courses, with differing titles, taught at a number of campuses, to diverse student populations. But I speak of the course as one and will refer to "it" rather than to "them" because I perceive the effort of teaching the literature of liberation as a single process with unity and continuity amidst a variety of forms. I suppose none of us ever teaches the same course twice. We're always revising, always adding this book and eliminating that lecture, introducing this film or field trip and letting go of what is for us a favorite reading but functions for the students as a fruitless struggle. I have not found the perfect combination of ingredients, nor do I expect to do so. I have, however, discovered and created a number of useful (because fruitful) ingredients.

The purpose of this paper is to describe those ingredients, reflecting on their value in a course on liberation thought within a religious studies context. My interest is twofold. Not only do I wish to outline the contents of the course; I wish also to describe some processes through which learning happens. It is this latter aspect, the learning process, which I am particularly eager to discuss when we meet. I look forward to your reflections and additions.

One of my goals as a lecturer and as a teacher is not only to be prepared but to be overprepared. Being prepared is an important response to one's commitments and I do not underestimate its value--often I struggle to meet it. But I find that being overprepared gives me more freedom to move in a variety of directions at a moment's notice and it affords a greater relaxation of spirit, enabling me to really listen to student questions and observations.

For this reason I rarely distribute a course syllabus the first day of class. Normally I have my own mental or rough-draft outline of how the course might be put together, but I wait until I have met with the students before putting type to ditto-master. I need to hear why they are there. I need to find out what questions they bring to the class, what moves them to register for this particular offering.

And so one of the items on the agenda for the first class meeting is to ask the students to respond in writing to one or more of the following questions:

> What prompts you to take this class?
>
> What questions do you bring to the course? Which issues do you wish to pursue?
>
> What are your hopes and expectations for this class?
>
> Complete the following sentence: The best thing that could happen to me in the course of this course is . . .

An alternative technique employed for the same purpose is to design and distribute a list of topics and authors and ask the students to indicate those of interest, adding any of their own that are not given. An example of what I mean follows, in greatly abbreviated form.

Interest-areas (check as many as perk your interest)

_____ social protest and civil disobedience

_____ racism

_____ violent and nonviolent strategies for change

_____ the Churches in Latin America

_____ sexism

_____ Dietrich Bonhoeffer

_____ Mohandas Gandhi

_____ Frantz Fanon

_____ Camillo Torres

(and a host of others)

There are several values in spending time eliciting student questions (or lack of them), interests, hopes and expectations. First, their responses to the questions or check-list begin to make these strangers real persons to me and reveal to me something of whom I'll be working with (and working for) during the coming weeks. Second, the exercise communicates an attitude of mind that is an important part of my own philosophy of teaching, namely, that they are active participants in the learning/teaching process we share and not simply passive recipients. Third, the activity provides a discipline for dealing with the question of why they are doing what they're doing, grounded in the conviction that it is better to be reflective rather than unreflective about one's choices. Some of the students admit that they do not know why they are taking the class, others claim they do not know enough to articulate any questions, and still others are quite clear about why they're there and what specific issues they wish to pursue. All responses are revelatory--both to them and to me--and in that sense, good to hear. There is no predetermined right or wrong. I simply want to know what's in them and I want them to know it, too. It soon becomes clear to those who are unreflective, however, that there are options open to them and that they might consider exerting more initiative in their educational experience.

I use these papers to give final shape to the course design and either distribute copies of the various questions that emerge or else I structure a discussion in which they inform one another of their intentions. In this way we are all a bit more conscious of who we are as a group and what brings us together. I keep the papers in my files for reference throughout the quarter and return them on the final day of class, with marginal markings regarding the realization of their original hopes. In this way, the exercise functions to give a certain unity to the course, for we spend part of the final class period in dialogue with the first class period, noticing to what extent we have realized individual and group goals, and to what extent we have surfaced previously unarticulated questions and achieved unanticipated understandings.

I place a great value on questions, agreeing with Suzanne Langer's comment (<u>Philosophy in a New Key</u>) that the questions a generation asks tell us far more about them than the answers they've offered or the discoveries they've made. I like to encourage students to notice their questions, to spend time with questions; I try to nourish their question-asking inclinations. And I see the fun and the frustration of teaching to revolve around what I call <u>the art of asking questions</u>. The challenge for me is to frame my question in a way that elicits their own, so that I can design a syllabus that honors and deals with their current questions at the same time that it stretches them into seeing and asking new ones.

Also, I often use the final day of class meetings to ask the students to articulate a response to the following:

> What questions, which have emerged in the course of the quarter, would you like to pursue further?
>
> or
>
> If we were beginning all over again, with ten weeks of study ahead of us, what questions would you want to pursue?

Again, responses to these questions often reveal a depth of understanding as well as, or perhaps better than, written papers and examinations. Furthermore, their responses alert them to avenues for further inquiry and study.

Readings   As you might predict, my selection of class readings varies from quarter to quarter. Paulo Freire's <u>Pedagogy of the Oppressed</u> has remained something of a constant, however, since its publication by Herder in 1972. I find it a remarkable book and I love to talk with people about it. Freire not only says a great deal about the processes of liberation, oppression, and consciousness-raising, about the demands and the pitfalls of the revolutionary leader, and about the goals of radical social change, but his work is also suggestive of a number of important themes not developed in detail. In this way the book invites its readers to consider a host of issues and to seek additional supplementary sources.

One of these undeveloped themes is the question of the means to make change happen. Freire assumes that violence is inevitable. This assertion prompts us to look at a variety of methods and to deal with concrete examples of both philosophies and strategies of violence and nonviolence. Another theme calling for further investigation is suggested in the preface where he states, "...this admittedly tentative work is for radicals. I am certain that Christians and Marxists, though they may disagree with me in part or in whole, will continue reading to the end." I see that remark as an invitation to spend time on the Marxist analysis of oppression and alienation. The comment also functions as an opening for dealing with diverse theological perspectives on the relationship between the Christian and the world. This latter theme in turn points us toward work done by Christians in Latin America—whether in the hills (Camillo Torres), in the pastoral ministry (Dom Helder Camara), or in the university (Gustavo Gutierrez).

42

A student once suggested that the next time I require Freire's book in a class, I use it in relation to B. F. Skinner's Beyond Freedom and Dignity. It seemed a good idea, and I followed her suggestion. Together these books sharply illuminated the differing humanistic and behaviorist perspectives on freedom and determinism. A take-home midterm examination assignment made this contrast particularly clear.

Exam

Write a review of B.F. Skinner's Beyond Freedom and Dignity from the point of view of Paulo Freire. Attach to this a brief response from Skinner.

or

Write a review of Paulo Freire's Pedagogy of the Oppressed from the point of view of B.F. Skinner. Attach a brief response from Freire.

The results of both class discussion and written examinations convinced me that the student's suggestion to deal with Freire and Skinner in dialogue was indeed a good one.

Other books assigned as required readings have included Gustavo Gutierrez' A Theology of Liberation and (when I have chosen to emphasize the processes of ethical inquiry) H. Richard Niebuhr's Responsible Self and Michael Novak's Experience of Nothingness. (Still other quarters I have had everyone read works by Martin Luther King, Frantz Fanon, Mohandas Gandhi, Malcolm X, the Berrigans.) Gutierrez' book was not well received by students the one quarter I used it. The Catholics in the group had a less difficult time with the terminology, but even they experienced a struggle which in the end did not appear altogether fruitful. This led me to conjecture that although it is a rich piece of research and reflection, A Theology of Liberation may function more fruitfully as a source book for the professor than as a required reading for students.

In addition to the common readings for which everyone is responsible, students are urged to pursue a topic of their choice such as the Black Movement, the American Indian, Mexican-American, or Women's Movements, and to engage in an in-depth study which complements as well as deepens the class sessions. I have put together bibliographies on each of these areas for student reference. Since several class periods are spent on what is meant by oppression and what diverse forms it takes (political, economic, educational, racial, sexual), it is important for the students to study a particular movement in order to recognize and to appreciate the unique historical and cultural experiences that differentiate movements one from the other.

A-V Materials   Films are particularly useful in making visual a number of points Freire makes. "The Land Burns" (Brazilian, 12 min.) graphically depicts drought, poverty, and death which immerse the lives of so many. "End of a Revolution?" (Bolivian, 26 min.) illus-

trates the powerful forces that are at work to prevent needed institutional changes. Films on political theater as an instrument for
consciousness-raising and for exploring alternative patterns of life
also complement Freire's discussion of education toward critical consciousness. "Gandhi's India" (58 min.) is a fine supplement to a
study of Gandhi's writings. A documentary on the life of Gandhi and
his influence on contemporary India, the film employs old news footage
as well as interviews with his associates and followers. "Why We Boycott" is a film on the Farm Workers' struggle in California and is a
graphic expression of boycott as a vehicle for social and economic
change. A (1963) tape recording of Kenneth Clark interviewing Malcolm X, Martin Luther King, and James Baldwin, and a record of Daniel
Berrigan reading selections of his poetry have continued to be such
useful additions to class readings and discussion that I am inclined
to collect audio-visual items with the same enthusiasm I have for col-
lecting books. Unfortunately the process is much slower since a-v
items never come in the form of free desk copies.

Guest Lecturers   Invited speakers enhance the class as well.
Professors Carlos Cortez, Chairman of the Mexican-American Studies
Program at UCR, and Laura Head of the Black Studies Program added
significantly to the class one quarter, speaking as they did from
their competencies as historian and as psychologist, as well as
their being members of the communities they reflected upon.

       One year (in Philadelphia) a police training corps from
New York City enacted a socio-drama in order to illustrate how the
police are trained to deal with potentially violent situations in
nonviolent ways. This presentation was a pertinent supplement to
our class discussions on thinking creatively about alternative responses in the midst of violent or potentially violent situations.

       Searching out additional ways to stimulate both thought
and discussion have continued to fascinate and frustrate me, and I
am always alert to the discovery of fresh and fruitful stimulants
for thought and discussion. I call such stimulants "starters" because they get students (and instructors as well) started in thinking
about certain issues and then discussing them.

Brainstorming   On several occasions I have used the process called
brainstorming as a way of urging students to think about their experiences of freedom and unfreedom. The process is similar to word-associ-
ation games. Participants can say whatever comes to mind. No judgments,
disagreements, or critical comments are appropriate. The point is to
evoke words or phrases that reflect understandings of freedom. I
function as recorder, putting on the chalkboard whatever students offer.
After five or ten minutes and a chalkboard covered with words and phrases,
we stop the brainstorming process. Now is the time for judgment. We
look at the total output before us and make observations about what we
see: certain words or ideas recur; people see freedom in diverse,
even contrasting categories; for some freedom is essentially a physical
state, for others a psychological or spiritual condition; for some,
freedom means opportunity (freedom for...), for others, freedom suggests absence of restraint (freedom from...). Etc. etc. etc. My ex-

perience has been that the discussion gains momentum as these observations are articulated and lively discussion inevitably ensues. The point of all this? The exercise provides a structured group activity, in which everyone participates, alerting us all to think about an issue central to the entire course.

Value Sheet   Another "starter" I have found useful is what Sidney Simon and colleagues call the value sheet, a sheet of paper listing six or eight descriptions of freedom (or topic of one's choice). Each student is asked to read the descriptions carefully, to choose which one best represents his or her own position, to modify it if necessary, or to write a new statement. The point is to find or to design a statement to which the student can say, this is where I now stand on this issue. Having dealt with one's own understanding of freedom, one is more alert to deal thoughtfully with a particular author's contribution. For a fuller discussion of the value sheet, see Values and Teaching by Louis E. Raths, Merrill Harmin, Sidney Simon (Columbus, O: Charles Merrill, 1966), ch. 6.

Contrasting Interpretations   To evoke judgments on the material students are reading, I have often juxtaposed contrasting interpretations of a particular thinker or a particular issue. A pertinent example is: "The Berrigans--Prophetic? (Richard J. Clifford) or Phrenetic? (Andrew M. Greeley)," Holy Cross Quarterly, vol. 4, no. 1 (January, 1971), 14-19.

Simulation Games   One quarter I used a simulation setting as an alternative to a written examination. The class was small and it seemed timely to find a fresh approach. The materials to be covered were the writings of Gandhi and Fanon. With sixteen students in the course it was possible to have them re-group into partners. I asked four pairs of partners (eight people) to assume the position of followers of Gandhi and the other four pairs (eight people) to assume that of Fanon. The directions given (to the pairs) follow:

> With your partner create a situation that demands a response; deal with the situation in a way that you think a follower of Gandhi would be likely to handle it. (The skit should be limited to two or three minutes.) Then when you have acted out the situation, you are to handle questions, observations, and criticisms from the rest of the class, speaking to their questions from within the position of a Gandhian as you understand it.

The same directions were given to the "followers of Fanon" substituting his name in place of Gandhi's.

As a substitute for a written examination, the simulation worked very well. Everyone participated fully, both by designing and enacting a skit and by posing questions to those on stage or by fielding questions from within the assumed position. In the process of it all, students were using, and not simply recording from memory, what they understood to be Gandhi or Fanon's positions. For a group larger than sixteen, the simulation would undoubtedly need to be modified in order to avoid the boredom of too much repetition.

I am convinced that simulations can provide valuable learning experiences, though this is an area I am just beginning to research. As this paper goes to press, I will be attending a four day
workshop on the use and design of simulation gaming for educational
purposes. Presumably I'll have more thoughts on this by the time we
meet for discussion in October.

<u>Evaluations</u>   I find written student evaluations of the course to
be generally quite informative and helpful and I always include them
as part of the final class session. Occasionally I spend some time
at the mid-point of the quarter encouraging evaluation of the course
as well. This structures reflection and feedback about how things
are going and it brings to consciousness the <u>process</u> of learning as
well as the content of learning. I think this <u>is</u> critically important,
and I find students surprisingly unaware of their own learning processes
and learning styles.

My departmental colleagues and I use the same evaluation form
and are interested in eliciting student judgment on three main points:
1) the strengths of the course and instructor; 2) the limitations of
the course and instructor; and 3) an assessment of their own participation as students. This third question reads, "How do you assess
yourself as a student in this class? To what extent did you commit
yourself through concentrated effort to making this class a fruitful
learning experience? What percentage of classes did you attend?"
The question is designed to prompt awareness of the students' role
in creating a worthwhile class and to counteract what is too often
a prevailing tendency to judge a course on the entertainment score
of the professor as performer.

The attached course syllabus indicates that the class is
based upon lecture sessions as well as discussion, film, guest visitors,
spontaneous written activities, research projects, examinations, and
simulations. My underlying hopes are several: to expose students
to a rich literature on a critical issue within a cross-cultural context, to offer a variety of activities for learning to happen effectively,
and to create an atmosphere where individual student concerns and rigor-
our academic research complement each other.

RS184b LIBERATION MOVEMENTS   J. O'Connor
T Th, 1½ hour sessions

        The thrust of this course is to discover and discuss to-
gether the religious and ethical dimensions of the human struggle
for liberation in the contemporary world. Paulo Freire's Pedagogy
of the Oppressed provides a point of departure for a consideration
of the processes of oppression, freedom, and liberation while other
authors exemplify more concretely the ways in which this struggle
takes expression in the Black, Mexican-American and Native American
communities, and in the Women's Movement.

        In addition to Freire's book, B. F. Skinner's Beyond Free-
dom and Dignity and Gustavo Gutierrez' A Theology of Liberation will
comprise the common readings. Individual student projects will involve additional readings pertinent to the movement of their choice
(Black, Chicano, Native American, or Women). Bibliographies on each
of these four movements are available.

        Hopefully this course will aid you in reading both carefully
and widely, in thinking deeply and expressing yourself clearly. You
are encouraged to engage in thoughtful, informed class participation.
There will be one or two quizzes covering the common readings (Freire,
Skinner, Gutierrez), and each student will design a project in con-
sultation with the instructor. This project may take the form of a
research paper or a bibliographical essay or a project involving
audio-visual media. You may have additional ideas. The final examination is negotiable.

                            Calendar

Classes

    1   Introduction; student hopes and expectations; overview
           of common readings, issues, possible directions for indi-
           vidual study projects.

    4   Lecture and discussion on "Third World" and "Fourth World";
           working definitions of "freedom" and "liberation" and "op-
           pression"; liberation as process; diversity of movements
           nationally and internationally; consciousness-raising.
           Class reading: Freire, Pedagogy of the Oppressed.
           Films: "The Land Burns"; "End of a Revolution?"

    2   Lecture and discussion on the behaviorist critique of the
           language of freedom; "pre-scientific" and "scientific" views
           of human life (autonomy vs. environmental controls); tech-
           nology of behavior; operant conditioning; long range goals.
           Class reading: Skinner, Beyond Freedom and Dignity.

    (Take-home quiz on Freire and Skinner)

    3   Lecture and discussion on the "theology of liberation";
           Vatican II; the impact of Marx and Freud on the literature
           of freedom and liberation; the Christian-Marxist dialogue;

the relationship between the Church and the world; Dietrich Bonhoeffer and the world "come of age"; liberation as salvation/redemption; toward a spirituality of liberation; theology of hope and the future.
Class reading: Gutierrez, A Theology of Liberation.

2   Lecture and discussion on the Black Movement: Malcolm X and the Black Muslims; Gandhi and King on the values of nonviolence; Fanon and the value of violence; Cone and the blackamerican theology of liberation.
Tape: Clark interview with Malcolm X, King, Baldwin.

2   Lecture and discussion on the Native American Movement; "red power"; AIM; Wounded Knee; Vine Deloria and God Is Red.
A-V presentation: "Indian Accounts of the Last of the Indian Wars" (Dr. Robert Hine, professor of history).

2   Lecture and discussion on the Women's Movements; R. Reuther and the theology of liberation; the relationship between black women and white women regarding oppression and liberation; women and the Churches; women and society; M. Daly and the attempt to go "Beyond God the Father" in creating a theology/philosophy of women's liberation; human liberation.

2   Lecture and discussion on the Mexican-American struggle; Cesar Chavez and the United Farm Workers.
Film: "Why We Boycott."

1   Guest speakers' panel presentation on the Black, Chicano, and Women's movements.

1   Where are we now and where do we go from here? Putting/pulling it all together; review and concluding reflections; course evaluation.
(Take-home quiz on Gutierrez due)

Student projects due in final form, the week of final examinations.

EDUCATION FOR WORLD JUSTICE:
FROM THE VIEWPOINT OF THE CHRISTIAN TRADITION

Introduction

The question of world justice touches all people; it is
not confined to one religious tradition, to one nation, one race
one sex. Its ambience includes the cultural, the economic and
the political dimensions of life as well as the religious.
Education for world justice is, therefore, not only a theological
task, but a study in depth requires the cooperation of many disciplines. This paper addresses the question of world justice
from the viewpoint of the Christian theological tradition, with
particular emphasis on the Catholic tradition. It does not
deal with this tradition as something fixed and completed which
needs only to be applied to concrete circumstances; its concern
is a living theology closely engaged with the socio-political
realities of our world, linked from the first with a world-wide
renewal of human life. It continually seeks a truer earthly
expression of the kingdom of God even while it knows the truth
of the old Huguenot proverb that, "there is no need of success
in order to persevere." [1]

A basic impulse to the writing of this paper has come
from my experience over more than four years in teaching theology
at the University level. Courses taught on the Church and
world development have convinced me of the urgency of "an
on-going process of education of all Catholics in the facts of
world justice and planetary interdependence." [2] Indeed factual

49

knowledge is not enough, but analysis, reflection and action
must accompany this education. Because the quest for justice
is closely related to a knowledge of the world, some study of
the political, economic and social fields is essential. This
includes special attention to the North American situation, because
without knowledge of the local picture, no concrete action is
possible.

As the hard realities of our world are studied and grasped,
it grows clear that, "We must love one another or die." as the
poet W. H. Auden wrote already at the time of the First World
War. 3 World justice can no longer be seen as the special work of
some. For the Christian it cannot be a mere addendum to Faith;
it is at the heart of Faith itself and a basic responsibility of
every believer. The quest for justice, therefore, plays a forma-
tive role in the entire theological enterprise, renewing theology
itself.

In the pages that follow, I will set forth some basic
aspects of a Christian theological education for world justice
under the following headings:

  I.   The Church's Call to Justice

  II. The Basic Conflict in the World Situation*
       and the Options Posed
 III. Strategies for World Justice

I. The Church's Call to Justice

World War II represents a watershed in human history. It
focused the attention of nations and of churches on the urgent
questions of justice and human rights, of peace and freedom in their
global dimensions.   Vatican Council II was a watershed for the
Catholic Church; a new relation to the world was stressed from
which there is no turning back. The radical confrontations at the
Geneva (1966) and Uppsala (1968) meetings of the World Council of
Churches have the same thrust.   These watersheds together with
the growing awareness that the entire world is faced with an
ecological crisis and that millions face starvation while others
live luxuriously have alerted many Christians to the urgency of
world justice.

The time is ripe and awareness has grown, yet the full impact
of the justice question has not come home to most Christians, whether
Catholic or Protestant.   Christian Faith has for too long been understood as a private affair; the large socio-economic dimensions of
life have been untouched for many years. The social vision of the
Church, of the Churches, is not known. One reason for this may be
the failure to communicate Christian teaching in concrete and vivid
ways that relate to human experience. Another reason may be the
sacrifice required to bring even a portion of this vision to reality.

Nevertheless, there is a long history to the Catholic Church's
teaching on world justice. The letter of Pius XI on Reconstructing
the Social Order (1931)[4] said things which can still shock. Few
Americans know that the Pope criticized capitalism severely, as a
system of ruthless competition, which gives to a few untold riches

and power while leaving the vast masses propertyless. The directives
of Leo XIII in the letter on <u>The Condition of Labor</u> (1891)[5] had
been forgotten or "deliberately ignored."[6] Neither the letter of
Leo nor of Pius XI has had a significant impact in the Christian
world.

Yet since the watersheds mentioned above, it is evident that world
justice and peace can no longer remain abstract, praiseworthy ideals;
they are a matter of life and death for humankind. As Bryan Hehir notes,
the question of justice is moving "steadily from the periphery of
the Church's life toward the heart of her life." [7]

The Bishops at Vatican II spoke of the huge numbers who live in
misery while others squander resources and live luxuriously. If the
poor nations are to survive, profound changes are needed in the rich
world. The Bishops spoke of technology which must be put to the
service of humanity's real needs, not used to multiply products
meaninglessly for the sake of profit.[8] Pope John spoke out in two
letters on social justice.[9] Paul VI's letter, <u>On the Development of
Peoples (1967)</u> followed.[10] Many Christians found this letter socialist,
if not communist, in tone. Paul spoke strongly against a liberal
capitalist order in which the key motive is gain, fierce competition
is the supreme law and ownership of the means of production is made
an absolute right.[11] This letter stressed justice, which requires a
structural change. The structures that oppress must be challenged;
individual charitable campaigns are grossly insufficient.[12] The time
for change is short; a note of urgency fills this letter.

A few years later came <u>A Call to Action</u> (1971)[13] Paul focused
on the growth of the multi-national corporations, which are under
neither national nor international control. The excessive power
already condemned by Pius XI takes on a more formidable character in

this new development. "Just principles and prophetic denunciàtions"[14] are not enough, men must work to change unjust structures. Christian groups cannot be neutral. The Church in all its people must awaken to its role at the international level. Development as envisaged by the capitalist system is also called in question.

Justice in the World was released the same year (1971) by the Synod of Bishops meeting in Rome. This Synod took a clear theological position: The work of justice and liberation is no mere follow-up of Christian faith, which falls to the responsibility of the few; it is constitutive of faith and the responsibility of all.[15]

Other decisive documents are: 1)The papers from the Latin-American Bishops'Conference at Medellin in 1968. The Bishops place the Church on the side of the poor and the oppressed in the revolutionary ferment of Latin America.[16] Up to this point, most Church documents have in reality been an appeal on the affluent world to change unjust relations so that the poor world may have a chance. A turn is present in these papers: Solidarity with the poor is stressed. Church leadership has yet to face the full meaning of this choice. Often it is hoped that all will work harmoniously, a unity that hides conflict and which may ultimately mean siding with the rich. To side with the poor is to allow division to arise; such conflict may lead ultimately to a truer unity, to a peace founded in justice. 2) Several other groups of Third World Bishops have spoken out: the Bishops from the Northeast of Brazil;[17] the Bishops of Peru;[18] the Bishops of Mexico.[19] 3) The Bishops of the United States have announced the theme, "Liberty and Justice for All,"[20] as central to the Catholic celebration of the United States' Bi-centennial (1975). A process

has been started which in three phases will continue to 1981,
to examine and act upon issues of justice and freedom in the United
States itself and in its relations to other peoples.[21]Finally,
the letter on Appalachia, This Land Is Home to Me (1975), a
regional letter which carries universal significance, marks a new
rich growth in the Church's vision of justice.[22]It inaugurates a
process that is linked to the poor in Appalachia, concerned with
grass roots' concrete problems, builds upon genuine study in order
to develop a comprehensive plan of action, and is grounded in prayer.

The direction of the Catholic teaching on justice over the past
eighty years, and especially in the last fifteen, is clear. A growing
commitment to world justice and liberation marks these documents.
Until the present, however, a certain ambivalence is found in these
teachings. Because the Catholic Church aspires to be the Church
of all, it often seeks a reconciliation without conflict. Yet it
hardly seems possible that structures of injustice will change
by maintaining neutrality. It is hard to take sides with the poor;
it requires deep change in the Church itself and in world systems.
But not to do so may ultimately mean to serve the status quo. The
next section will analyze this point.

II. The Basic Conflict in the World Situation
and the Options Posed

A study of our world with special attention to the North American
situation is the second basic theme of an education for world justice.
What are the conditions in which our world finds itself? If we
affirm that all human beings have basic rights, such as the right
to work, to eat, to be educated, to have a say in one's destiny,

ultimately the right to/relationship to other human beings and to
                       ^grow
God,[23] we know that our world reveals situations of bitterness and
conflict that abrogate these rights.

The socio-economic-political structures, questioned in the
Church documents, have their main power base in what is called
the First World which comprises the North American and Western
European countries especially; this is mainly a white world and
is of Christian heritage. The peoples wounded by this power
are mainly in Africa, Asia and Latin America, which is called
the Third World. Pockets of the Third World (the poor minorities)
are present in the rich societies; rich oligarchies are present
in the poor world. A study of the Second World, the Russian bloc,
is also necessary, but it cannot be encompassed in this paper;
generally speaking, it too belongs to the affluent world.[24]

A grave source of conflict is the great and growing gap between
the two-thirds of the world's peoples who are poor and the one-third
that is rich. Actually a Fourth World is appearing, "the world of
despair,"[25] which has almost no chance for survival. In analyzing
this conflict, a myth must be cleared away. Many believe that the
misery and poverty of the Third World is due to ignorance, to
laziness, to mindless over-population.[26] It is forgotten that world
trade relations are on the side of the powerful and that the market
economy serves the strong. The pattern which existed for more than
four hundred years under colonialism is continued today under neo-
colonialism.

The poor countries, often dependent on one crop or one mineral,
a pattern developed under the domination of the past colonial powers,
cannot bargain as equals with the rich countries. The last three
meetings of the United Nations Conference on Trade and Development (UNCTAD)[27]

give evidence of this. At the conference table the rich world
consistently refused to build fair trade relations. The myth
mentioned above hides the true reality. The affluent world is
not helping the poor; its riches depend in great part on the
labor and resources of the poor. Truly understood, the poor
work for the rich at starvation wages. Nor does it seem likely,
as many have thought, that the pie will be shared with greater
justice by further development along capitalist or Russian socialist
lines. The First Development Decade inaugurated by the United Nations
was a failure; the Second Decade gives little promise.[28] In actual
fact the rich world is now doing less for the poor world than it
did earlier.

This grave conflict between the poor and the rich is aggravated
by the juxtaposition of the environmental and population questions,
which are only now being grasped. It is gradually recognized that
development according to the Western norm is impossible to share;
the world would become unlivable from pollution.[29] At the same time,
we know that the world's population will be about seven billion by
the year 2000 and that most of this growth will be in the Third World.
Some genuine growth and development is essential for a minimally good
life, even for survival itself.[30]

This new dimension of conflict is at once complicated and
threatening. To affirm the needs of people will increase pollution
and kill the environment; to affirm environmental needs is to
condemn people to a less than human life. Some in the affluent
world would say, "Let the poor starve; they are having too many children."
But it is not a matter of population alone; it is a matter of

consumption. At the U.N. Population Conference in Bucharest
(Summer, 1974) Rene Dumont spoke of the "rich white cannibals" [31]
and said that the Third World should unite against them. The
great discrepancies between the poor and rich countries are well
documented. A New York Times article on population said,
"Developed countries with one-third of the world's population
consume about 60 per cent of energy production and the use of other
basic commodities is similarly disproportionate." And again,
"A person in a developing country may be lucky to get a pound of
grain or its equivalent a day. In the advanced nations, per capita
consumption is five times that." [32]

The growing gap between poor and rich breeds anger and despair.
The earth's resources are limited; this is the heart of the matter.
The richer world speaks out immediately for a reduction in population.
But the poor world says the main problem is the greedy consumption
of resources and the pollution of the world by the rich lands. The
Conferences at Bucharest and at Rome revealed the polarization.[33]
Food and material go not to those who have the greatest need, but to
those who can pay the most, because the profit motive holds primacy.

Yet, despite this deep and angry conflict, the environment
and population questions affect everyone ultimately. The realization
is growing that "we are all under the ax. All of us are likely to
be doomed or saved together."[34] There is Only One Earth,[35] and we are
all interdependent. This can, perhaps, be understood as a sign of
hope rather than despair. It may move us to build a sharing world,
a sharing community, rather than a fiercely competing one.

What Are the Choices Set Before Us?

There would seem to be three basic possibilities:
The affluent world could force its will on the poor, in order to
secure its own riches, even if this should mean wars of domination.
The poor world could wreak havoc on the rich by new and more daring
forms of guerrilla warfare, led by desperate human beings willing
to die themselves in order to obtain some share of the earth's
bounty for their people.[36] These choices tend towards death
rather than life.

Is there on the other hand a possibility that human beings
will choose life that is grounded in a universal love? This would
mean social justice for the great multitudes of people on the earth
who are now poverty stricken and starving. But this is not possible
without a basic change in the people of the rich world, i.e. in the
style of life, and without a transformation in the social, economic,
political and religious frameworks. Is there any hope for such
a 'de-development'[37] of the affluent world, or at the very least a
'very different kind of development.'

Can the people of the United States, who are so dominant in the
First World, make this choice for life and for world justice? It seems
almost impossible, but the other options only lead to chaos. This
choice would require bold measures: a deep change in the American
set of values and in the economic structures which stress unlimited
growth, competition and which value success as the final criterion
of human worth. It would require the re-shaping of democracy, the
giving of power to the powerless, the valuing of economic equality
as well as political equality.[38] This choice would challenge the
Churches to side in reality with the poor and oppressed, rejecting

all complicity with vested interests that bolster injustice.

To expect the Churches to side with the poor seems at first sight quixotic and even partisan. Yet it becomes clear in the situation we are facing, that if we do not take sides with the poor, we take sides with the rich and have the consciousness of the rich. There is no neutrality.

The great middle class of America, the wage earners,[39] are of special importance if this option for world justice will be taken. Education for world justice from the Christian theological viewpoint must be especially addressed to them. Although many are the descendents of poor immigrants, they are at present on the side of the rich rather than on the side of the poor world. They are not themselves the policy makers, nor the wealth owners in society; yet they are the beneficiaries of a system which exploits the Third World. This fact is often hidden from their eyes, but it influences their attitudes, values and moral sensitivities.

This large body of the American people is Christian by heritage. Can the Christian Church if it moves to the side of the poor give them a place to stand that is wider than the love of self and the love of one's own kind of people? Can the remembrance that they are, in great part, descendents of the poor help? Can the awareness of the world's interdependence, for life or death, help them to choose life for others and ultimately for themselves? Can the knowledge which dispels/societal myths that cloak injustice be an aid, the 'truth-force' (ahimsa) of which Gandhi spoke? [40]

It is not possible now to know the answer to these questions.
The choice for social justice is essential. It would be unrealistic
to believe that such a choice would be clear-cut from the first and
achieved by the mere exercise of the will. Yet there exists in the
human heart a longing for real community and there is God's promise
that all/persons are meant for a life in which mercy, justice, joy and
friendship are fundamental. It is therefore not impossible to
hope that this choice may be made.

Strategies for World Justice

The importance of an education for world justice and peace
which raises men's consciousness and moves to action cannot be
underestimated.   In addition this education must reach great masses
of people, if it is to have an impact.   How can this be accomplished?
especially in relation to the American scene?

Three basic points in relation to the study of the world would
appear to be of first importance in any model of education:[41] A
thorough and wide knowledge of the needs of the poor and the oppressed,
that is, of the Third World both at home and abroad;   a knowledge
of the relationships between the rich and poor nations, concrete
factual understanding of the unfair trade relations that exist; third,
and most important, a growing awareness of the needs of the affluent
world itself, and of its need for liberation.   Many Americans today
are aware that something has gone wrong and that the quality of life
has diminished. Extensive consumption and material comfort does not
satisfy and it is possible to recognize as never before that "Man
does not live by bread alone." [42] A competitive society geared to
unlimited production works against solidarity and community, so that

human beings are alienated from one another and friendship cannot
grow deep. The way of the affluent hurts not only the Third World;
it imprisons the affluent world itself in an environment which is
rich in material things, but poor in joy and community. Added to
this, there is a growing awareness among many Americans that they
have little real control on the large economic-political institutions
that shape their destinies. The freedom to consume exists, but not
the freedom to control.

This third point is akin to the 'conscientization' emphasized
by the South American educator, Paolo Freire.[43] The injustices which
hurt the poor, ultimately hurt the affluent also, and life tends to
lose its meaning. For its own sake, therefore, the affluent world
needs to recognize its collaboration in injustice.

Traditional models of education can make good use of these
three basic points. For the Catholic, a knowledge of the Church's
call to justice, together with the work of Christian political
and liberation theologians can help people realize that they are
not alone, that there is a tradition in the community of faith which
can sustain them, even as this tradition itself grows and develops.

New models of education are, however, needed. Powerful methods
and ways which help to open human hearts so that persons may perceive
at greater depth and confront with hope the grave situations which
face the world today. New models of education which combine
theory and practice, reflection and action are essential. Many
examples can already be found in American society: the Community
Service Organization of Saul Alinsky;[44] Bread for the World, the newly
formed Christian citizens' movement on hunger and poverty;[45] the
grass roots groups of Network (founded by the National Association

of Women Religious),[46] the many small groups throughout the country
which have worked closely on the boycott with the United Farm Workers.[47]

One model of education, however, needs special study for the
task that lies ahead. Perhaps the most significant question as
regards an education for justice is: How can human beings achieve
the political will that is needed for the immense task of building
a new society and a just world order? This challenge is posed at
a difficult time; human beings are now asked not to share their
surplus, but to share their necessities or scarcities. Human beings
are inclined to take care of their own needs first, forgetful of the
growing world of despair. We have seen that either the violence of
the strong or the subversive violence of the powerless can erupt from
this. Without erecting non-violence into an absolute, is it possible
that non-violent movements, in the tradition of Gandhi and M.L. King
may be the special road for white Americans in the decades ahead? [48]
Non-violence not as an individual sortie, nor as a merely passive
stand, but rather non-violence as a revolutionary method, as the
violence of the peacemaker, as a campaign and strategy directed toward
specific, yet often diverse, goals.[49] A non-violence that has energy
"for the long march through the institutions"[50] and courage to resist
powerful vested interests. Non-violence, understood as a method and
campaign which engages genuine personal commitment is a model of education which is not in any sense individualistic or elitist. It demands
personal sacrifice and dedicated leadership, but its aim is to reach
everyone, helping to create the way to justice that is rooted in the
heart yet built -in to the structures of society.

In Conclusion

An education for world justice that stands in the Christian
tradition requires faith and it should lead ultimately to a
deepening and renewal of Christian faith itself. Work for world
justice can seem an impossible task. The world today is more
structured and organized than any human person of the past has
known. The individual can feel her/himself powerless before the
mighty structures that encompass her/him on every side. Courage
to go on despite failure, courage to persevere over the long
haul depends ultimately on God's aid and help.

Jesus Christ has revealed the God who has drawn near to men,
who stands on the side of the poor, the oppressed and the outcast.
This Jesus died for all men as a criminal outside the walls of
Jerusalem, because he mingled with the despised and the prostitutes.
His central message is the promise of the Kingdom; God's promise
that human life is meant to be a life in solidarity, giving glimpses
in this world of the love that extends beyond death. As Christian
men and women educate themselves in world justice through reflection
and action, anchored in the presence of the Spirit, all the great
symbols of Faith can be understood anew and at greater depth. The
letter on Appalachia, This Land Is Home to Me speaks of this
possibility for the Church, the community of Faith. The letter
concludes by expressing the hope that by pursuing justice the

"Church might once again be known as

- a center of the Spirit,
- a place where poetry dares to speak,
- where the song reigns unchallenged
- where art flourishes
- where nature is welcome

      - where little people and little needs come first,
      - where justice speaks loudly,
      - where in a wilderness of idolatrous destruction
        the great voice of God still cries out
        for Life." [51]

Mary I. Buckley
Asst. Professor of Theology
St. John's University
Jamaica, New York 11439

June 1975

NOTES

1. Quoted by W. R. Coats, God in Public (Grand Rapids, Michigan: Eerdmans, 1974), p.199.

2. Barbara Ward, The Angry Seventies (Rome: Pontifical Commission for Justice and Peace, 1970), pp. 70-71.

3. Quoted by R. McAfee Brown, Religion and Violence (Philadelphia: Westminster Press, 1973), p. 100.

4. Pope Pius XI, "Reconstructing the Social Order," (1931) Five Great Encyclicals (New York: Paulist Press, 1939, pp.125-67.

5. Pope Leo XIII, "The Condition of Labor," (1891), Ibid.,pp. 1-29.

6. Pope Pius XI, op. cit., p. 142.

7. Bryan Hehir, "Ministry for Justice," Network Quarterly, Washington, Vol. II, No. 3, Summer 1974. First page.

8. "Vatican II, Church in the Modern World," Documents of Vatican II, edited by W.M. Abbot, S.J. (New York: America Press, 1966),272-3.

9. John XXIII, Peace on Earth (with commentary) (Glen Rock,N.J.: Paulist Press, 1961); Mother and Teacher,(with commentary) (New York: America Press, 1963).

10. Paul VI, On the Development of Peoples, with commentary by Barbara Ward (New York: Paulist Press, 1967).

11. Ibid., pp. 44-45.

12. Ibid., pp. 37-38.

13. Paul VI, "Octogesima Adveniens," (A Call to Action, 1971) The Pope Speaks, Washington, D.C., Vol XVI, 1971-72,pp. 137-64.

14. Ibid., pp. 158-159, 162.

15. "Justice in the World," Crux Special (Albany, N.Y.: Clarity Publishers, 1971), p.1. Copy of document used for this paper.

16. For the official English translations, see The Church in the Present-Day Transformation of Latin America, Vols. I & II, edited by Louis Michael Colonnese (Bogota, General Secretariat of Celam, 1970).

17. "I Have Heard the Cry of My People," by 18 Catholic bishops and major religious superiors of the Northeast of Brazil, May 1973, IDOC North America, New York, No. 54/Summer 1973, An IDOC Extra.

Mary I. Buckley
Asst. Prof. of Theology
St. John's University
Jamaica, New York 11439

18. "Closing Statement of the 36th Peruvian Bishops' Conference," 1969, in Between Honesty and Hope, Translated by J. Drury (Maryknoll, N.Y.: Maryknoll Documentation Series, 1970).

19. Statement of Mexican Bishops in late 1971, reported in Justice in the World, a primer for teachers, Module 7 (U.S.C.C.: Washington, D. C., 1972).

20. "Liberty, justice will be themes of bicentennial," in National Catholic Reporter, Vol. 10, No. 33, June 21, 1974, p.1.

21. Liberty and Justice for All, A Discussion Guide (Washington, D.C.: U.S.C.C., 1974),pp. 5-6.

22. This Land Is Home to Me, text put out in newspaper form by the Catholic Committee of Appalachia, 31-A South Third Ave., Prestonsburg, Ky., Executive Director Rev. John Barry.

23. Paul VI, On the Development of Peoples, op. cit.,p. 33, pp. 49-52.

24. At the Bandung Conference in 1955, the world of capitalism and the world of communism were seen as the first and second worlds, respectively. The uncommitted nations who wished to be independent and who were poor saw themselves as a third world. The terms are misleading today, but convenient.

25. "Interview with Dom Helder Camara," IDOC North America, New York, No. 54/Summer 1973, p. 16.

26. E. Toland, T. Fenton, L. McCulloch, "World Justice and Peace: A Radical Analysis for American Christians," IDOC North America New York, No. 54, Summer 1973, The whole article describes six societal myths that hide the truth.

27. H. Camara, Structures of Injustice (London: Justice and Peace Commission, 1972), p. 2 and p. 39.
and B.V.A. Roling, "Poverty, Conflict and the Emerging Ecocrisis," Papers from the Club of Rome Symposium in Holland, 1972, IDOC North America, New York, No. 52, April 1973, A Special Issue, p. 45.

28. Ibid., p. 46.

29. R. Heilbroner, An Inquiry into the Human Prospect (New York: W.W. Norton &Co., 1974), pp. 31-58.

    B.V.A. Roling, op.cit., p. 47.

30. "Population Boom and Food Shortage: World Losing Fight for Vital Balance," The New York Times, Aug. 14, 1974, p. L 35.

31. "Positions Polarizing over Population Issues," The Christian Science Monitor, Vol. 66, No. 191, Aug. 26, 1974, p. 2.

32. New York Times article, op. cit, p. L 35.

33. <u>Christian Science Monitor</u> article, op. cit.

34. J. M. Swomley, Jr., <u>Liberation Ethics</u> (New York: Macmillan,1972),p.l

35. B. Ward and R. Dubos, <u>Only One Earth</u> (New York: Norton, 1972).

36. R. Heilbroner, <u>op. cit.</u>, pp. 40-46, p. 79 and p. 81.

37. See the important article, "De-developing the United States through Nonviolence by W. Moyer, Papers from the Club of Rome Symposium, <u>op. cit.</u>, pp. 61-67.

38. <u>Poverty in American Democracy: A study of social power</u> by the Campaign for Human Development (Washington,D.C.: U.S.C.C., November 1974). It reveals the powerlessness of the poor and the working class despite the fact that they can vote.

39. J. C. Raines, "The Middle Class: Unmasking the American Myth," <u>Christianity and Crisis</u>, New York, Vol. 34, No. 6, April 15, 1974, pp. 73-77. This article does not speak of a middle class but of the difference between wealth owners and wage earners.

40. M. K. Gandhi, <u>Non-Violent Resistance</u> (New York: Shocken) published by arrangement with Navajivan Trust, Ahmedabad, 1961. pp. 40-42 and 91-92.

41. J. Barndt and G. Hrbek, "International Consciousness: Education for Awareness and Action," article in <u>Education for Justice</u> (Maryknoll, N.Y.: Orbis Books, 1975) This article has been helpful in outlining the three aspects.

42. R. Heilbroner, <u>op. cit.</u>, p. 70.

43. P. Freire, <u>The Pedagogy of the Oppressed</u> (Herder & Herder: New York, 1970). <u>Education for Critical Consciousness</u> (New York: Seabury Press, 1973).

44. Saul Alinsky, <u>Rules for Radicals</u> (New York: Random House, 1971).

45. <u>Bread for the World</u>, 602 East 9th Stree, New York, N.Y.

46. <u>Network Newsletter</u> and <u>Network Quarterly,</u> Washington, D.C.

47. P. Matthiessen, <u>Sal Si Puedes</u> (Escape If You Can) A biography of C. Chavez the leader of the United Farm Workers.

48. R. Mc Afee Brown, <u>Religion and Violence</u>, op. cit. See the last chapter.

49. W. Moyers, "De-developing the United States through Non-Violent Campaign ", <u>op.cit.</u> Stresses the important of campaigns.

50. From Rudi Dutsche, the Student leader of Berlin West Germany, who was later shot but was not killed. The phrase may come from H. Marcuse.

51. Last Page of Appalachian letter, <u>op. cit.</u>

THE USE OF "BASIC ASSUMPTION" PROCESS GROUPS IN THE
TEACHING OF RELIGION: A REPORT[1]

Charley D. Hardwick
The American University, Washington, D.C.

        This paper reports a particular experiential teaching method in religious
studies which grew out of group dynamics theory. Many attempts to adapt experiential techniques to religious studies have long impressed me as artificial, and,
whatever other pedagogical merits they have, I have wondered about their effectiveness in promoting understanding in the study of religion per se. The most effective experiential techniques (games, role playing, simulation models, sensitivity
training laboratory exercises, training groups) seem to be those where there is
a direct and intimate relationship between the subject matter being studied and
the content of the experiential exercises. I am thinking, for instance, of courses
in psychology, sociology, international relations, political science, management,
and clinical practicums in which the very content of the learning concerns such
issues as roles, modes of group task functioning, power relations or social
differentiation.

        The work of W. R. Bion [4] and Philip Slater [12;13] has suggested that
there are remarkable and wide-ranging analogies between processes which develop
in the evolution of certain kinds of small groups and archaic religious processes.
If there is merit to Bion's and Slater's hypothesis, then these "small study groups"
can be used directly in religious studies teaching. The artificiality I have
spoken of would be overcome because the relationship between experience and subject
matter would coincide exactly with that which justifies the most successful
experiential teaching, and the classroom could be transformed into a laboratory
for the study of religion.

        When I discovered the work of Bion and Slater some years ago, I was
nearing the completion of training as a "consultant" in the Bion or Tavistock
method of process group study. I had initially undertaken this training for
reasons having nothing to do with my own field and with no particular thought to
using it in the classroom, so the possibility opened up by Bion and Slater came
as a burst of illumination to me. I immediately set about designing a course in
social scientific theories concerning the archaic roots of religion. The course
has now been taught five times, and I have continued to have a broad experience
with process group study in contexts outside the study of religion itself. Despite
my excitement at "discovering" the idea for this course, I realize there was
nothing original in it. Variations of the "process group" model for religious
studies teaching have been used widely in recent years and long before I began.
My purpose in making this report is to raise issues for discussion, not to make
a claim for originality. There are also certain distinctive features of the
Tavistock model which, to my knowledge, have not been reported in the context of
religious studies. These features lead to certain methodological and theoretical
questions about Slater's work which I shall discuss near the end of this paper.

                              THE MODEL

        According to well established group dynamics theory there are sometimes,
perhaps always, "hidden agendas" operative in groups. These are processes and
interactions underlying or paralleling the "overt" rationale which has brought
the individuals in the group together. They can, so to speak, only be caught out
of the corner of the eye. These are (1) group processes in that they cannot be

reduced simply to individual behaviors. And they are (2) <u>covert</u> in nature in that they are other than and hidden from the acknowledged purposes of group activity and are only vaguely, if at all, recognized by group members. Group study seeks to develop methods whereby individuals can experience and learn about these covert processes as they occur. There are a number of such methods and a number of theories about the nature of the processes which occur and the uses to which this learning can be put.

The Tavistock method developed from the work of Henry Ezriel and W. R. Bion [4;5;6;7]. It is based on psychoanalytic theory as this was extended into group dynamics by Bion's "basic assumptions" hypothesis. I will not elaborate Bion's theory except to say that he regards basic assumption activity as an attempt to deal with primitive fantasies occasioned by anxiety provoking situations in a group. Bion defines three basic assumption postures which can occur in a group: (1) fight/flight; (2) dependency; and (3) pairing. What is impressive about Bion's model for the study of religion is the archaic and non-developmental character of the group processes which the theory conceptualizes. This material is archaic because it deals with primitive fantasies shared in the group, and it is more or less non-developmental because, as Bion says, there is a timeless quality about the basic assumption activity and these processes can recur at any stage in group life.

The problem for any group dynamics model is to create an environment in which distinctively group processes can emerge and be dealt with (studied) in their own right. In the Tavistock method, a group is brought together and given the express task of studying its own behavior in the here and now. (The size of these groups can vary, but for the purposes here I shall confine myself to the "small study group" the outer limits of which are 12-14 members.) Such a group is provided with a "consultant" who has two role tasks to which he adheres rigorously. He sets the time and space boundaries of the group by acquiring and arranging its meeting place and by arriving and leaving precisely on time. And he makes comments about the here and now processes occurring in the group at such times as he believes opportunities for learning will be made available to the group. As a result of these role boundaries, the consultant has a peculiar status in the group. He sits, so to speak, on the boundary of the group. He never becomes a group member (though assiduous efforts are made by the group to make him one), but because he continually intrudes upon the group by his interpretive activity, he can never be treated as though he were absent, invisible, or merely a neutral observer (though again the group often behaves as if any or all of these were true).

Although such groups have a task or an "agenda" (to study their own behavior in the here and now), the felt experience at the inception of such groups is precisely the reverse. And this is the intention of the model. The day to day conventions by which "agendaed" group activity is conducted are suddenly stripped away; a group of strangers find themselves placed in a situation which is felt to be chaotic, engulfing, goalless; and the "authority" who created the situation frustrates all the learned or fantasied expectations about how a "teacher" or "leader" is supposed to behave and is instead experienced as silent, unmoving, and depriving. The result is an extraordinarily high level of anxiety which is defended against by resort to rigid and stereotypical behavior based on primitive fantasies shared in the group. This in turn manifests itself in massive "transference" phenomena which, at least near the beginnings of such groups, but also long afterwards, is directed upon the consultant. Indeed, the "blank," "authority," "inside/outside" role of the consultant is designed to elicit and to receive this transference. (The application of psychoanalytic transference theory to group phenomena may seem an unwarranted theoretical construction to some, but it is well attested in the theoretical literature. [Cf., 5;6]) As these transference phenomena are interpreted by the consultant, it is hoped that group members will become more skilled at seeing and understanding these "covert" processes themselves. This assumption alone justifies the use of this method in academic settings rather than solely in therapeutic ones.

The primitive character of the transference material as well as the psycho-analytic theoretical framework which permits one to interpret it as primitive are what attract me to the Tavistock model as a method in religious studies. "Primitive" or "archaic" are, of course, notoriously slippery concepts. By them I mean, follow-ing Slater, a situation prior to the development of culture. As Slater says, such groups "approximate in a few respects what a group might be like in the absence of culture. This is of course a matter of degree--training groups are highly sophisti-cated pieces of civilization, but they are artificially impoverished with regard to certain crucial cultural products" [13:767]. This meaning of "primitive" thus approximates in highly suggestive ways to both psychoanalytic and anthropological theories concerning the roots of culture, and it is significant that at least some of these conditions can be recreated in microcosm in the classroom. Students have opportunities to observe the psycho-social origins of religion in experiences of chaos, maternal engulfment, primitive attempts at individuation, and the Oedipal dependency structures through which such attempts play themselves out [12 passim]. As the group develops, they also have opportunities to observe in their own group life the development of "cultural" forms analogous to the religious expressions by which reactions to these primitive processes are embodied: the construction of a world; the maintenance of social cohesion through the elaboration of group myths and sacred texts; deprivation, powerlessness, and dependency; the reactions of scapegoating, sacrifice, rebellion, and aggression followed by continued ambivalence, guilt and the quest for atonement; apocalyptic catastrophe and messianic hope; "the sacred," sacralization, mystification and demystification.

It must be noted, of course, that the phenomena which occur in such classes are not "religious" in any immediate or direct sense. They can be viewed as religious only from the perspective of some social sciences interpretive framework which seeks to dissect the archaic roots of religion. This approach would there-fore be questionable for those approaches to religious studies which seek to treat religion as a phenomenon sui generis. In any case, I try to make clear to students in these courses that religion is being studied within a social scientific frame-work and that the objective of the course is to help them experience and then interpret the connection between the archaic constituents of religion and religion itself. Students who cannot make this distinction and then see the connection find the course ultimately frustrating, and it fails in its religious studies goal for them.

In my attempt to adapt this model to a course in religious studies, the Bion method is rigorously adhered to. The reasons for this, and the pedagogical problems it occasions will be discussed below. All class sessions except an opening orientation and a closing review and evaluation are conducted as a process group with myself serving as a consultant to the group. All of my interventions in the class are interpretations of here and now group processes. I make no specific effort to color my interpretations with religious ideas--although any group studies consultant will often find that "religious" imagery is the most natural vocabulary in which to phrase certain statements. Other than my interpretive interventions, which at times are rare, I give no formal directives for group development. It is made clear to group members that they may say or do anything they wish during group sessions. These groups are consequently experienced as lacking a formal task and as having no group goals, and I am treated as a depriving authority figure. This is so despite the fact that all group members are informed on several occasions that the task of the exercise is to study here and now group behavior and to relate it to theories regarding religious development drawn from the social sciences.

I limit the class size to thirteen members. While I require no prerequisites, I do insist upon an individual interview with each student as a condition for entrance to the course. This serves two purposes. First, I inform each student thoroughly of the unusual classroom procedure and its rationale. I take pains to explain the religious studies context of the course. I stress that the religious studies goal and its method of achievement are more cognitively complex than the typical study group exercise since an additional element of learning is grafted to the pedagogical purpose of the usual study group (the purpose of which is to learn about group process), and I try to prepare the students themselves to make this connection. Finally, I make clear that this method of learning is frustrating and at certain points generates considerable anxiety. I use the interview, second, to discourage some students from taking the course. These are either students who are actually seeking psychotherapy or those for whom the stress conditions of this kind of exercise would be personally threatening. Identification of these students is much easier than might be expected--a few minutes of conversation suffices--and discouraging them can be done tactfully and indirectly. Usually a careful description of the nature of the model, its religious studies goal, and an emphasis on the anxiety generating feature is enough. This interview also has the advantage from the student's side of allowing some, for whom there are no personally disqualifying reasons, nevertheless to self-select themselves out of this kind of course in advance if for any number of reasons they find it does not meet their needs. I want to emphasize how important this early selection process is. The model is sufficiently powerful (and dangerous) that it would be irresponsible to permit indiscriminate enrollment when it is used in an academic setting. Prerequisites will not meet the problem, so it is necessary to erect enough artifical barriers to make possible selection by the instructor and self-selection by the student.

I draw up a detailed syllabus in which all I have previously said about the model and its goals is presented at length in writing. At the first class session, I go through the syllabus, thus repeating the content of the earlier interview, and discuss specific points with the students at length. If students express an interest at this first meeting, I do not hesitate to discuss the group dynamics theory behind the model. I go to such lengths to orient students to the exercise because, as mentioned above, this attempt to adapt the group studies model to religious studies is cognitively complex. It is difficult enough to experience and study covert group processes. It is doubly difficult to relate these chaotic, anxiety-ridden experiences to complex psychoanalytic, anthropological, and religious theories. Nevertheless, as anyone experienced with training group methods will know, prior didactic preparation seems to have little effect at all. Once into the experience, groups seem to develop a massive amnesia, experience the group as formless and without a task, complain of the competence of a teacher who could have designed such a course, and monotonously reenact the same behaviour patterns and strategies from group to group for dealing with their anxiety. Still, this didactic framework is important because it is one of the boundaries which holds the exercise

within an academic framework, and as the group becomes more skilled at understanding here and now processes, it serves as a kind of touchstone to which the group
can return and around which understanding can begin to concentrate in about the
second half of the semester. In Slater's terms, it is an "external" element which
can help break through the ethnocentricism which would characterize a therapy
group but which is intolerable in an academic setting [12:254f.].

       At the end of the syllabus, a reading list is attached with specific reading
assignments and dates for their completion. Given the nondirective character of
the teacher role in this course the order of these assignments is only my recommendation, and students may complete the reading list in an order and at times of their
own choosing. The reading list moves from classical but general sociological and
psychoanalytic theory about religion to a set of psychoanalytic interpretations of
specific mytho-religious traditions and finally to a set of readings in group
dynamics theory and its relation to religion. The last weeks of the course are
devoted to Slater's Microcosm.

       The scheduling arrangements at·my institution require that group sessions
(class meetings) be held either once a week in a two and one half hour block
(which I divide into two segments with a ten minute break) or twice a week in
one hour and fifteen minute blocks. Neither of these arrangements is ideal. The
most dramatic transference material and the most dynamic developments of "boundary
consciousness" occur in groups which come together often and thus sustain a critical
level of intensity and continuity. Groups which cannot meet frequently undoubtedly
experience a "dilution factor." (This problem can be surmounted in once a week
groups but only if they have a group life much longer than is possible within the
constraints of course credit systems and academic calendars.) In particular, I
find that the longer the breaks between meetings the more difficulty such groups
have with group depression. This means not merely that they tend to get stuck in
the dependency basic assumption and have difficulty working themselves into what
Slater calls "the group revolt." More seriously from the Tavistock perspective,
it means that they have more difficulty in evolving to a point where they can
begin to have some understanding of the group processes they are undergoing. My
most successful class from a dynamic standpoint was one taught during a five week
summer term in which it was possible to meet for an hour and a half five days a
week. Fortunately, a new˜schedule at my university will make it possible for me
to offer this course in the future with three one hour sessions per week on
alternating days during the week. While this factor of frequency of meetings is
not overriding, consideration of it should enter into the design of such courses
where possible.

ASSESSMENT: PROBLEMS AND PROSPECTS

       Before I address myself to the rather obvious pedagogical problems of this
course design, I want to begin by saying I am enthusiastic about it and plan to
continue to experiment with it in the future. With very few exceptions, my students
have been excited by the classroom model and often return long afterwards, having
had an opportunity to integrate the learning opportunities this method makes
possible, to report its value. Despite the problems I shall address in a moment,
I have clear evidence from journals the students keep that as much reading and
understanding goes on in this course as in others taught by more traditional
methods. (This is, of course, not necessarily saying much, but it is an important
perspective to have in mind as I move to the assessment which follows.) From a
religious studies standpoint, there is evidence that a considerable amount of

"impicit" or "tacit" learning occurs, particularly near the end of the semester when Microcosm provides a framework which pulls together the disparate theoretical material worked through earlier. In addition, the Tavistock model is designed to emphasize problems of authority, leadership, and responsibility. Consequently, whatever its strengths and weaknesses as a method in religious studies, a spin off of the course is that it enables students to deal directly with a whole set of experiential issues concerning the nature of learning and their own responsibility for it. Specifically, it helps many students see their own complicity in the passivity generated by more traditional methods. This is a contribution of the course which is not to be gainsaid and is perhaps warrant enough for continuing to offer it.

Nevertheless, the central pedagogical problem with this course will already have become evident to you. There is no place in the course design where the theoretical materials which justify the course are self-consciously and systematically treated in the classroom itself. The experiential element and the theoretical literature simply run parallel to each other. In particular, the design does not permit the "instructor" to assume his normal obligation to help students understand a body of theory and apply it to data. There is no question that the course produces a considerable amount of raw data which lend themselves to "religious studies" interpretation. In this sense, the design is an admirable research vehicle. But doubts must be raised concerning whether it can accomplish its pedagogical goals.

Of course, the design does clearly permit--even demand--that students in the course themselves take responsibility for bringing the theoretical material into the class sessions. Theoretically there is no reason why this cannot occur, but in practice it seldom works out very well. In the first place, in groups such as this issues of boundary definition, differentiation, interpersonal distancing, and transference are so powerful and overwhelming that for long periods of their history there is "no time" to work on any other material except that having to do directly with group development itself. Furthermore, it is precisely the transference issue which often works in such a way as to create a group taboo precisely against bringing any theoretical discussion into the group sessions, and individual students who make the attempt either receive no support or are punished severely. Just as in the traditional classroom, students often deny their own competence in a self-destructive strategy to sabotage a professor/authority. Of course, this activity is always interpreted, and eventually this produces considerable enlightenment about group processes in the classroom. But it does not solve the problem of achieving the religious studies objective in the midst of the experiential exercise itself. In other words, one must ask whether students can learn anything from the model except about group processes and thus whether its use in religious studies is legitimate.

In journals and in papers written near the end of the semester, a small number of students do show a surprising competence in understanding the theoretical literature and applying it to their classroom experience, and with a few others the theoretical lights go on some time after the course is completed. (The analogy to the methodological problems of acculturation in anthropology is interesting and significant.) But neither of these exceptions meets the problem of achieving the religious studies component more directly in the time devoted to classroom work. With almost all students there are clearly varying degrees of "tacit" learning [10] that occurs directly in the experience itself--as a consultant one sometimes has the uncanny sensation that there is a kind of "secret gnosis" being passed around

in the group--but it is almost impossible for a group to verbalize this learning
in any coherent or sustained fashion.

I am not prepared as yet to judge this model a failure because of this problem of wedding experience to understanding in the classroom. I have tried to focus
it with some acuity, however, because it is not unique to this model alone but will
occur with any experiential teaching technique. I am still sufficiently undecided
myself about the nature of experiential learning, about the model itself, and about
the legitimacy and limits of tacit learning in a university setting to want to keep
the issue open at this time. Several modifications or additions to the design
might be tried (confining enrollments to more advanced students, making a course
in theory a prerequisite, interlacing didactic sessions with experiential ones,
etc.), but in the interest of discussion here I want to limit my remarks to the
single alteration in the model which raises the most complex methodological questions. This will serve the purpose of relating my model to Slater's work.

This would be to alter the model so that the "consultant" took a more active
role in introducing theoretical material into the group sessions, thus insisting
by his own example that the group engage the religious studies element in the
design. This is the point at which differences between the Tavistock model and
American training group methodologies become relevant. I have already indicated
that I believe the group study model requires that the consultant adhere rigorously
to a task role in which he does nothing more than make interpretations of here and
now group processes. This has the consequence of leaving to the group members the
sole responsibility of making the religious studies application. One might well
ask, then, how Slater seems to have succeeded with such brilliance.

First, it should be noted that Slater's work is a theoretical construction
of a body of data drawn from a series of study groups he conducted. He never
presents the pedagogical context or rationale for these groups. It is at least
implicit that these groups were not offered as courses in religious studies. One
can derive from his work no more than the point I have already made, namely, that
study groups are an admirable vehicle for research in religious studies. Second,
Slater has almost nothing to say in detail concerning his "teacher" practice in
these groups. In his transcripts of group material, one can occassionally "read
out" something of his practice, but at just this point certain ambiguities begin
to appear. On the one hand, his discussion of the revolt phenomenon assumes a
precise Tavistock group model and consultant role: a group "lacking formal
procedures or rules of order" "with no assigned formal task and no clearly defined
group goals" having a "formal leader [who] gives no directives" and who is consequently "a source of deprivation for the other members." [13:766f.] On the
other hand, Slater at times suggests that he played a more directive "teaching"
role by introducing material for discussion, encouraging the group to "stay to
the point" by exploring its ramifications, and himself following it up with his
own contributions. This "teacher practice" would conform more closely to American
training group models, and Slater does at times seem to rely heavily on the work
of Mills [8;9] and Bennis and Shepard [2].

It is indeed significant that Slater uses the word "leader" to describe his
role. In the training group model, the teacher does function more as a leader
by providing a model of "good" group membership which encourages members to explore
issues of openness and trust with one another and thereby move the group toward
more effective, democratic task performance. As Klein and Astrachan note in their
admirable essay comparing the two models:

T-groups characteristically have a trainer who uses his authority to demonstrate the kinds of behavior which help the group create conditions conducive
to "good" group work. The trainer therefore behaves in an open manner,
owns up to his own feelings, asks for and gives constructive feedback, and
limits his comments to data generated within the group. Trainers are primarily interested in helping members immediately apply what is learned in
the group. . . . [The] trainer attempts to act as an accessible authority
figure, openly owning up to his own feelings and acknowledging his behavior.
Within this framework confrontation is possible and members may then inter-
act in a more supportive, collaborative, trusting manner. . . The trainer
rejects the role of an impersonal "rational" voice and models the role of
a good group member. The T-group trainer is aware that the members of the
group have invested him with phantasied authority, but rather than fostering
its growth, he attempts to use his authority in order to define the work
of the group. [7:670f.]

By contrast,

The study group consultant behaves in an idiosyncratic way, he attends only
to his own task, but because the members invest him with authority, they
begin to follow his example and to see his behavior as forcing theirs.
Authority is ambiguous and is thus subject to scrutiny. The T-group trainer
deliberately utilizes his authority in order to get the members relating
to one another in ways which modify the hierarchy and allow collaboration.
The trainer thus truly leads, that is, he guides and indicates and in this
process the authority which was initially invested in him by the member's
phantasies now becomes legitimized. . . . The study group ideally provides
a setting in which one can develop "insight" into the functioning of the
group. This technique is based upon psychodynamic theory, with the assumption being made, that by examining transference issues, one ought to develop
insight into functioning and then have the freedom to change. The T-group
provides a setting in which appropriate behavior can be modeled and the
assumption is made that one learns by developing new concepts and then
having the opportunity to practice new skills and behavior. [7:672]

Slater himself gives the game away when he describes his exercises as "groups in
which candor, self-revelation, insight, and the expression of feeling are strongly
and explicitly valued" [13:766f.]. While the Tavistock consultant does present
a design which makes clear that an exploration of feelings will be important, he
makes every effort not to value, support, or model group behavior but rather to
interpret it and thereby to provide opportunities for learning for which each
group member must assume his own responsibility.

    I certainly do not want to argue for the superiority of either of these
methods. Each has its own strengths and weaknesses and its own uses in the
university. I do want to raise the question whether they can or should be mixed in
a religious studies design. The strength of the design I have presented is the
archaic "religious" transference material it elicits. My experience with training
groups has been that transference material is ignored in the interest of developing
different, and quite legitimate, group learning. This point in no way calls into
question Slater's achievement. But his theoretical construction of group material
could have drawn its data from either model. My question regards the pedagogical
design for a course in religious studies. In this sense, it is by no means clear
to me that modifying my design into the training group model would solve the problem
I have presented.

THEORY

In conclusion, I want to present two theoretical points about Bion's and Slater's work to which my experience with these classes has given rise. I am not prepared at present to do more than suggest these issues, but I hope they might lead to some discussion and further research.

The first point concern's Bion's basic assumptions hypothesis. Probably the weakest point in his discussion is his attempt to apply the basic assumptions postures sociologically. He does this by drawing analogies between covert small group processes and institutions which mobilize them. He thus associates fight/ flight with the military, dependency with the church, and pairing with the aristoc- racy (!). By these rather wooden analogies, Bion neglects the much more interesting sociological implications of his hypothesis which have to do with the structural components of any and all social phenomena. From this perspective it might be possible to show how all the basic assumptions are operative, but differentially organized, in any form of social organization or interaction. In any case, Bion does unfortunately imply that the religious analogy applies only to the dependency basic assumption and then institutionally only to the church. I want to suggest here that there are a number of analogies to religious processes in all the basic assumptions and there are manifold ways they can be construed on the basis of group process data. This is not an original suggestion on my part since Slater makes rather a lot of the same point in his theory of group development [12:131- 250]. But Slater has by no means exhausted all the possibilities. For instance, he relates pairing to "secularization" in his scheme of group development. He also notes that pairing processes often occur around issues of group death and mourning. He does not, however, examine the interesting connections which may exist here in the history of religions to apocalyptic and eschatological phenomena and to the difference between historical and non-historical religions. Exploring such further analogies between all the basic assumptions and religious processes should be a fruitful area for further research.

My second point concerns Slater's developmental hypothesis. Slater's immense contribution is to have wedded Bion's basic assumptions to a developmental hypothesis which nevertheless gives proper weight to the non-developmental char- acter of the basic assumptions. He achieves this with his notion of a continuum of "boundary consciousness" in which there is an overall group development from bonds that are almost entirely unconscious (fusion) to those that are more and more conscious (demystification of the consultant, differentiation of interpersonal boundaries, greater reality testing). The basic assumptions can then be seen as strategies which serve different defensive purposes depending on the kind of boundary consciousness present at any given time; their "timeless," non-developmental quality derives not from the lack of group development but from the fact that they are all attempts to "freeze" a moment occasioned by anxiety into a state of equilibrium between engulfment or total isolation. Slater terms this process a development toward "secularization," and he then makes an ambitious effort to re- late these processes to theories of cultural and religious evolution—with partic- ular reference to Bellah's work [1].

Slater's argument is quite simply the most impressive addition to group dynamics theory since the path breaking work of Bion [4] and Bennis and Shepard [2] and I do not want to detract from his achievement here. But my own work with groups suggests that his theory needs further consideration and refinement. I can only adumbrate the reasons here, but I hope to present a more complete discussion to this group in the future.

The problem concerns the conclusions that can legitimately be drawn from Slater's notion of a development toward "conscious bonds," both microcosmically and macrocosmically. There is no denying that some such development occurs--in study groups if for no other reason than time spent together produces a group culture where none existed before which is based on interpersonal bonds, both conscious and unconscious, actually existing in the group rather than on the pure fantasy material present at the inception of a group; and macrocosmically based on increasing structural differentiation as elaborated by well known theories of cultural evolution. But some parts of Slater's discussion slant the meaning of this development in a certain direction. With small groups, he sometimes implies that there will be a decrease in basic assumption activity or at least that it will lose much of its archaic quality.[2] Then at the macrocosmic level, he implies that the development of greater differentiation carries higher rationality in the psycho-social foundations of social and cultural interaction [Cf., 12;3]. Religiously his use of the term "secularization" suggests either a decrease in religious activity or at least, with greater individuation and "multiplexity," a lessening, again, of its archaic features.

Stated with such bluntness, these points do a grave injustice to the full complexity of Slater's theory since he himself surrounds it with so many careful qualifications. He acknowledges the dangers in making any generalizations about the chaotic processes which occur throughout the life of a group beyond specific here and now interpretations. He notes that there is no such thing as "progress" in group development, that any gains are only temporary, that groups move in a crablike or inchworm fashion, and significantly, that "the 'basic assumptions' may . . . occur at any time and any order" [13:776]. He even has difficulty sustaining his argument about the group revolt. He tries to construe it as a turning point in the life of groups leading to his developmental hypothesis, but his own transcripts document its almost universal irresoluteness, the continuing occurrence of variations of revolt themes right up to the very end of groups, and the intensity of ambivalence, guilt, and dependency issues which surround them. At the cultural level, Slater notes the pitfall in any developmental theory which treats empirical entities as units on an evolutionary scale instead of analyzing them into components manifesting various archaic, basic assumption mechanisms which are then agglomerated in different combinations in the entity as a whole, no matter what its stage of cultural evolution.

All these qualifications are well taken, but once they have been added to the theory does Slater's point permit anything more than the much less ambitious and prosaic point that all groups experience some development of boundary complexity? Certainly I have observed this development in my own groups, and it is Slater's notion of the development of a continuum of boundary consciousness that has been most helpful to me since Bion's theory leaves one at sea on issues of group development. But I observe no lessening basic assumptions activity in this development and I am hesitant to accept any construction of these processes which suggests a dilution of their archaic features. Extreme caution must be exercised also, I believe, about how the notion of secularization is used to describe these processes. In particular, I am suspicious of any theory which suggests that greater differentiation (secularization in a minimal institutional sense) entails diffusion of higher rationality throughout the structural foundations of the entire social system. However we finally construe secularity, we have all too ample evidence from modernized societies that the archaic is not so much eliminated as differently distributed [Cf., 11].

Slater's problem derives, I believe, from a "valency" which he gives in his total discussion to his most condensed statement of his theoretical innovation. Discussing the seeming incompleteness of Bion's hypothesis, Slater asks "whether the three 'assumptions' do not really represent two different levels of conceptualization: that on the one hand they are simply points on some sort of continuum, but at the same time they also express different techniques for responding to or coping with the phenomena to which this continuum pertains" [12:169]. The valency in Slater's theory is toward an emphasis on the first phrase in this statement. Here continuum tends to be construed in a temporal sense with developmental stages, and despite himself, Slater cannot help but imply developments from "irrational" to "rational," "archaic" to "modern." The result is that "the development of conscious bonds" comes to imply the disappearance of unconscious processes. In contrast, when Slater is most astute, the emphasis falls on the second phrase. Here the continuum is construed more like a logical matrix in which the basic assumptions occur, singularly and in various combinations, as mechanisms with different strategies depending on developments of boundary consciousness. This emphasis is much more complex since it permits acknowledging a temporal dimension (a differentiating boundary consciousness) without requiring overly simplistic evolutionary stages which ignore continuing archaic processes.

My own work with study groups confirms this second "valency" which I believe needs to be given to Slater's condensed formulation. In agreement with Slater, for instance, I also find that a "pairing" culture usually (but not always) develops only after a group has had time to work up to a certain level of boundary complexity. Such a culture usually develops around issues of ending, death, and mourning. But it can also develop quite early as a defense not so much against engulfment as against disaster, against the terror of group dissolution when omnipotent fantasies about the expected achievements of the experience are disillusioned. On the other hand, there have been occasions near the end of groups (and quite contrary to Slater's evidence) when a strong pairing culture develops and then suddenly seems to combine with material suggesting the fight/flight basic assumption. Here, however, the fight/flight mechanism has altered from its "feel" in nascent groups. Instead of being a terror of engulfment (fusion with a shared unconscious) it expresses the alluring attractions of maternal envelopment, a dramatic experiential combination of the messianic hope for a deathless new aeon of sibling equality and mystical union with the Body of Christ.

The point I am suggesting about Slater's theory would allow one to take better account of such phenomena. It would, however, require a refinement in the meaning of "conscious bonds." Slater can speak of the development of boundary consciousness as an exchange of unconscious bonds for conscious ones because he seems to limit the notion of unconscious bonds to issues of fusion. An emphasis on the second construction of his condensed theoretical statement implies, however, that the relation between unconscious and conscious bonds is a continuing and more complex one even as "conscious bonds" (i.e., differentiated boundary consciousness) develop. This is the line along which further work should be conducted with Slater's theoretical model. Indeed much of the material for it is already present in his work (e.g., his use of transference theory), and he has himself shown his sympathies for dynamic psychology.

It may well be that the theoretical issue I have attempted to develop here is itself another reflection of the differences in group studies methodology discussed above. Klein and Astrachan mention that there is some significance to

the fact that the two methods developed in different sociohistorical contexts.
Sharing the same larger European cultural background as that in which psychoanalysis
originated, British psychoanalysts developed the study group method in an ethos in
which "character is viewed as developing slowly and stability of personality is
stressed." There is much greater concern for authority relations in the culture
as a whole, and "since the model depends on insights developed in the transference
to the consultant (who is a surrogate parent, employer, lover, sibling, teacher,
Godhead, etc.) change within members is seen as a very slow process which goes on
long after the group ends." The method tends consequently to proceed slowly and
cautiously and is suspicious about identifying developmental trends. The training
group method, in contrast, developed in an American setting and partially as a
reaction against European totalitarianism. It stresses "democratic structure
and interactions" and the culture it develops shares with the larger American ethos
the optimistic assumptions of infinite possibilities of change and the plasticity
of personality. "T-groups, therefore, emphasize the positive, stress observable
change, . . . and reject the analytic with its more negative view of change . . .
The trainer reinforces new behavior patterns and minimizes etiological and irrational factors." [7:665-667] Klein and Astrachan are careful not to draw value
judgments from these differences in background; the whole purpose of their essay is
to highlight the strengths and weaknesses in each method. But my own biases will
already have become clear. When we think solely in terms of theory and seek to
adapt group dynamics to the study of religion, we overlook the archaic at our peril.

FOOTNOTES

[1]A sample syllabus will be available at the meeting or will be provided by
mail upon request. Please enclose stamped, self-addressed envelope.

[2]Note, for instance, Slater's description of the substitution of conscious
bonds for unconscious ones: "Frank discussion of similarities and differences
between members, of likes and dislikes, attractions and repulsions, has been
substituted for the unconscious collusion of silence, of polite superficiality,
of avoided topics, of passive dependence on the leader. General complicity in
perpetuating some tedious intellectual discussion has given way to examination of
the ambivalent feelings it symbolizes. Unconscious 'agreements' (i.e., joint
actions created by individuals who sense each other's similar fantasies and ways
of viewing interpersonal relationships) to try and make of the group a battered
troupe of oppressed and victimized children, or a phalanx of brave soldirers, or
a mass society in which delicate and sensitive spirits are brutalized or go
unrecognized, or a rivalrous family in which the good little (bad little) older
(younger) male (female) child finally wins its rightful place to exclusive
possession of a parent, give way to an exchange of similar and disparate experiences
and the feelings produced by them." [12:244f.]

REFERENCES

1. Bellah, R. N.: "Religious Evolution," indem, Beyond Belief (New York: Harper
   and Row, Publishers), 1970.
2. Bennis, W. G., and Shepard, Herbert A.: "A Theory of Group Development,"
   Human Relations, 9: 1956.
3. Bennis, W. G., and Slater, Philip F.: The Temporary Society (New York:
   Harper and Row, Publishers), 1968.
4. Bion, W. R.: Experiences in Groups (London: Tavistock Publications, Ltd.),
   1961.

5. Ezriel, Henry: "Experimentation within the Psycho-Analytic Session," The British Journal for the Philosophy of Science, 7: 1956.
6. Ezriel, Henry: "A Psycho-Analytic Approach to the Treatment of Patients in Groups," The Journal of Mental Science, 46: 1950.
7. Klein, E. and Astrachan, B.: "Learning in Groups: A Comparison of Study Groups and T-Groups," The Journal of Applied Behavioral Science, 7: 1971.
8. Mills, T. M.: "Authority and Group Emotion," W. G. Bennis, et al, eds., Interpersonal Dynamics (Homewood, Illinois: Dorsey Press, Richard D. Irwin, Inc.), 1964.
9. Mills, T. M.: Group Transformation: An Analysis of a Learning Group (Englewood Cliffs, N. J.: Prentice-Hall), 1964.
10. Polanyi, Michael: The Tacit Dimension (Garden City: Doubleday), 1966.
11. Rubenstein, Richard: After Auschwitz (New York: The Bobbs-Merrill Co., Inc.), 1966.
12. Slater, Philip E.: Microcosm (New York: John Wiley and Sons, Inc.), 1966.
13. Slater, Philip E.: "Religious Processes in the Training Group," Donald Cutler, ed., The Religious Situation 1968 (Boston: Beacon Press), 1968.

THE JOURNAL SYNTHESIZING ACTIVITY

Zev Garber

Los Angeles Valley College

Of the many aspects of learning process, perhaps the most frustrating is the cross purpose of students and professors. No where is this more keenly seen and felt than in an introductory class. The professor's lectures are for the most part not understood, and his intelligence is further insulted by the student's seeming anti-intellectualism. The professor blames his failure on his young charges. He vents his disatisfaction by popping quizzes, assigning busy work, asking trick questions on exams, and springing a host of other tricks which only his mind can issue. Students become apathetic, turn off, and consider class attendance a punishing jail sentence.

In reality the problem grows out of the diversified roles played by the professor and the student. The professor sees himself as a knowlege dispenser, developing a new generation of scholars who share his philosophy and concerns, and are willing to spend infinite hours reading, researching, writing, and discussing the problems at hand. The average student does not have the scholarly way as defined by the professor. He is a tradesman interested only in the bare essentials of the job; how, when, where, what is required of him to obtain his grade. He could not care less about schools of thought, philosophy, sociology, history, literary analysis, and theoretical abstractions; he is interested only in the here and now.

The nature of a college program, introductory classes in particular, is such that a professor does not trust his student and a student does not trust his professor. Students are regimented through a structured program which gives them little time to reflect, think, and mature. No wonder passivity and inertia set in. To rectify this problem the professor could help his student understand the beauty of being a professional and not a mere worker. One of the ways in which this can be done is to change the nature of the written assignment. In place of hourly examinations, mid-terms, and finals, which often represent the scribbled jottings derived from a lecture hour, there can be the journal synthesizing activity. The major pedagogical principle gained is the students will learn better and appreciate more their understanding of the subject matter if they are actively involved in learning rather than being passively taught. Learning involves not only information given but the recipient's discovery of what that knowledge means. The journal synthesizing activity enables the teacher to be less of a knowledge dispenser, and more of a knowledge facilitator, who leads the student to make discoveries and articulate values and conclusions.

84

The journal is intended to combine aspects of the formal essay
with that of a diary. The entries are short exercises, five typewritten
pages are recommended, though there is no limitation on length. Activities
associated with lecture topics are written up as a journal entry and turned
in during the weekly class session at which the related topic is being discussed. The activities are many and varied, and provide an opportunity for
the student to develop methodology and preserve or alter deepseated comit-
ments in his view of himself, society, nature, and history.

Using topics from a Jewish Religious Heritage class, the following journal activities can be ascribed:

Topic 1 - Getting Started

Journal Activity: Students are asked to write their own definition of what is religion?; what is Judaism?; and who is a Jew? Included
in this statement, is the students' understanding of Jewish identity
viv-a-vis forces which seek to oppose or compliment it.

Topic 2 - Preliminaries About Religion and the Nature of Judaism
Journal Activity: Evaluate the mythic structure of classical
Judaism against the traditional view of Israel's origins and
destiny.

Topic 3 - Cycle of the Jewish Year: The High Holidays and the Nature
Festivals
Journal Activity: Visit a synagogue, or a place of Jewish
worship during the Jewish High Holidays (in the Spring semester, a
Passover Seder). Participate in a religious service (worship or
meditation) or have conversations with a member of the religious community. Describe your experiences in a journal entry.

Topic 4 - Cycle of the Jewish Year: The Minor Holy Days and the New Holy
Days
Journal Activity:
Construct your own Jewish Holy Day. What is its message, identi-
fying symbols, and meaningful rituals.

Topic 5 - Sacred Time and Sacred Space: The Shabbat
Spend 24 hours in a total Shabbat atmosphere, totally cutoff from
the everyday experiences around you, by participating in either a Hillel
Shabbaton (conventional, experimental) or a Chabad Shabbat (traditional,
mystical, Hasidic). Evaluate your encounter, citing both positive and negative effects. What new outlooks, if any, upon life have altered or emerged
as a result of the Shabbat experience.

Topic 6 - The Wheel of Life: Birth, Adolescence
Journal Activity: Make up a myth about the "beginnings of Israel"
or create an alternate rite of passage to the Bar-Bat Mitzvah.

Topic 7 - The Wheel of Life: Marriage, Death
    Journal Activity: Do a form critical analysis of the Jewish
marrige ceremony. Or attempt to write a responsa on one aspect of Jewish
marital relations and situation ethics. Or describe your thoughts about
death and the great "beyond." Or survey Jewish burial practices and philosophy with those of non-Jews, and write a rationale on the Jewish way of
dying. Or depict "death on my terms" using verse, poetry, visual arts, or
fiction.

Topic 8 - Master of the Universe: The Still Silent Voice
    Journal Activity: Describe an experience of the "death of God."
Or of God's absence. Or of the eclipse of God. Or of a self-limited God.
Or of an embattled God. Or of God in search of man.

Topic 9 - The Good Life: Man and the Human Predicament
    Journal Activity: Go out into the field and make contact with
one type of Jew Without Hope, e.g., the Jewish aged and dying, the Jewish
poor, the Jewish runaway or addict, the Jewish retarded or mental sick, etc.
Write up your experiences in a meeting-by meeting report. Be sure to
include personal data on your subject, description of the state of your
subject, progress made or needs being met, etc.

Topic 10 - Choose Life: The Jewish Ethic

Journal Activity: Comment on the following statement, either defending it or attacking it:

> The moral law of the Gospels asks the "natural man" to reverse his natural attitude towards himself and others, and to put the "other" in the place of the "self" --- that is, to replace straightforward egoism by inverted egoism. For the altruism of the Gospels is neither more nor less that inverted egoism. Altruism and egoism alike deny the individual as such all objective moral value and make him merely a means to a subjective end; but whereas egoism makes the "other" a means to the advantage of the "self", altruism does just the reverse. Judaism, however, gets rid of this subjective attitude entirely. It's morality is based on something abstract and objective, on absolute justice, which attaches moral value to the individual as such, without any distinction between the "self" and the "other" (from Ahad Ha'am, Between Two Opinions 1910).

-Or-

Discuss the Jewish view of Man and Nature in light of the following remark:

> In history there are three possible relationships of the spirit to the elemental forces. The first is the glorification of the elemental forces as such. We may call it the state of heathnism in the development of peoples, though there never was a pure heathenism in history. The second is the conquest of the elemental forces, the most illustrious example being Christianity. The third is the hallowing of the ele-elemental forces: not their glorification or conquest but their sanctification and consequently their transformation. The most striking instance of this relationship in the history of the Western World is Judaism (Martin Buber, from an adress delivered at the Lehrhaus in Frankfort-on-the-Main in 1934).

Topic 11 -   Torah: Tradition and Commentary; Continuity and Change
Journal Activity: Write an evaluation of the textual readings in this section: explicate the author's arguments; include a list of questions needing to be clarified or pondered; and a list of issues suggested by the readings appropiate for class discussion or activity.

Topic 12 -   Holy, Holy, Holy: Liturgy, Institutions, Diet, Dress

Journal Activity: Prepare a questionaire of at least ten questions on the role of the Synagogue or of Kashruth in Jewish life. Interview at least 15 informants: collate the answers and tabulate the results.

-Or-

Investigate the Tay-Sachs questionaire which can
be obtained from hospitals, Jewish community centers
or synagogues. What are some of the historical, cultural, and social dimensions behind the survey?

Topic 13 - Hashoah - The 614th Commandment: "It's O.K. To Cry..."

Journal Activity: Create a sociodrama (simulation, role
playing, etc.) entitled "The Last Jew Alive". Present at least five different views of Jewish belief
in the post-Holocaust future. Use section readings
and class lectures as a starting point.

-Or-

Make a collage of headlines from daily newspapers,
dramatizing the history and/or complexity of the issues
studied in this unit.

-Or-

View and analyze two media resources (e.g., the films:
"Night and Fog", "The Garden of the Finzi-Continis",
"The Shop on Main Street", "The Pawnbroker", or the
plays: "The Deputy", "Incident at Vichy", etc) on the
destruction of European Jewry.

Topic 14 - Encounter with Israel: People, Land, Destiny, World

Journal Activity: Write an essay or develop a short
story around the theme of Israelis and Jews, the
continuity (or discontinuity) of an identity. After all is said and done, what are the demands of
the God of Israel upon the State of Israel?

Topic 15 - Hear O' Israel: Plural Models of Jewish Identity

Journal Activity: Hand back students' definition of
religion and Judaism and ask them to reconsider
the statements in light of their encounter with
the course structure, lectures and readings.

The journal project permits a direct encounter of student
with material; leads to a variety of student-oriented class activities
and breaks up the doldrum of a lecture-only method of presentation.
The depth, variety, nature and breadth of the Jewish experience is
forcibly brought home if the student pursues his own journal preference in whatever media he deems most productive. For example, the
confrontation of old-world, shtetl values with American values, the
dilemma of the second generation, caught between the old values and
the new, the question of Jewish radicalism and what happens to it in
America, the question of Jewish "survival" in America, and finally,
the sharpening of the question "what is a Jew?"as Americanization
process continues can be portrayed in verse, poetry, music or photo-
graph. If done properly, the journal activity can weave a thread of

continuity into complex and diversified material and make the course
content more particular and personal.

The journal activity takes seriously the four sequential steps
of a learning process: Confrontation, where the student experiences the
idea, behavior, or object superficially; Analysis, where the student seriously probes the occasion or object in light of previous experience and
knowledge; Interraction, where the student's mutual or reciprocal communication with others helps him benefit from their feelings, ideas,
experiences with the reality under discussion; and Internalization, where
by turning the new experience and sharing of ideas upon himself, the student reacts meaningfully to the new reality as it relates to him as an
individual, and as a member of society as a whole. The journal activity
deals in the main with real life situations and not theoretical abstractions; it permits the student to confront deep philosophical ideas in
remarkable simplicity and convincing application; many new avenues of
knowledge are opened up since the student relies heavily on field research
in his confrontation with the subject matter and the problems at hand;
students develop sensitivity and learn empathy when they work with living
informants; finally, values, commitments, aspirations, etc., can be last-
ingly changed or developed or discovered when a student is engaged in
researcher-subject ethical decision making and moral development, the twin
pillars of a journal synthesizing activity.

The journal activity is less painful than many other writing
methods in deepening one's understanding of the richness of minority
history, culture, and contributions. It harmonizes the course curriculum
of subject matter and activity, of subjects of study and experience. As
a venture in human experience, it can prove more popular than historical
reading in fashioning meaningful, lasting ties in the appreciation of an
ethnic minority. It provides a more vivid and intimate insight into life
than does a textbook. A text must generalize but a journal entry is
personal and intimate. In addition, the student-researcher gives a different dimension of what "human awareness" means than is found in the
"heavy" findings of an anthropologist, theologian, historian, social
scientist, etc.

In sum, a journal synthesizing activity probes different bodies
of theory about phenomena, depending on the problem solving purposes. The
merits of a journal entry are evaluated on the basis of its content, simple
or complex, and also in terms of its aims and goals. For example, the
prospectus of a journal activity in the Jewish Religious Heritage class is
constructed to obtain the following major goals: (1) to be aware that
the Jewish religious tradition has to deal with peoplehood, worldview,
and life style; and (2) to realize that the culture, religion, and history
of the Jewish people are mutually interdependent. Furthermore, it is possible to reject an activity if the theory upon which it is based is not
accountable in demonstration and this it shares with other teaching
endeavors. Thus, a journal activity in the validity of the Halachic proces
is not possible, but as an illustration of Halacha it is acceptable. In
effect, a journal activity does not offer solutions to problems, but rather
a modus vivendi, in which different viewpoints may compete for acceptance,
and in the end be implemented though not receiving total support by all.

        Examples of journal activities done by students in the
Jewish Religious Heritage class taught at Los Angeles Valley during the
academic year 1974-75 will be handed out to those in attendance at the
Academic Study of Religion Section of the AAR on Saturday, November 1,
from 2-5 p.m. The selections will be discussed in light of the rationale
of a journal synthesizing activity mentioned above and in accordance with
the appendix, a section from the Human Awareness Program Guide published
by the Office of Instructional Development, Los Angeles Community Colleges
(August 1974). Also, a select bibliography in the study of the ethnic
minority will be handed out.

APPENDIX

The following are examples of specific concepts and historical developments pertaining to a college Human Awareness Program
published by the office of Instructional Development, Los Angeles
Community Colleges, (August 1974):

a. Concept of culture
    1. Social and psychological factors in development of culture
    2. Effects on personality and perception
    3. Value system: norms, beliefs, behavior
    4. Unity and diversity in cultural patterns
    5. Dynamics of change
    6. Cultural institutions
    7. Race, ethnicity, nationality, religion
b. Themes and issues in American History
    1. Development of minority and majority groups in the United
        States
    2. The melting pot versus cultural pluralism
    3. Distribution and utilization of power
    4. Distribution of poverty and affluence
c. Effects of discrimination on racial, ethnic, national origin
    cultural and religious groups in American society.
    1. Institutional aspects: schools, government and legal
        systems, news media, business and economy, religion
        the arts, community and public attack.

After the introduction of concepts and historical developments participation in practical field assignments of similar experiences to allow interaction with racial and ethnic groups is recommended. These activities should relate to the following:

1. Definitions of equal education as related to school and classroom
2. Assessment of students' abilities and achievements
3. Differences in student learning styles
4. Teacher, family and societal expectations of students
5. Self-image of students
6. Concepts of desegregation, integration, and pluralism as
   related to the school and classroom
7. Role models
8. Experience in wider community, including observation of
   community organizations and how they function
9. Militancy and activism in the community
10. Conflict between different minority and ethnic groups
11. Structure and governance of schools
12. Curriculum and instructional materials
13. Communication modes and skills of students
14. Self-image assessment of participants with particular
    reference to intergroup concerns
15. Observation of successful teachers and their methods

PUBLIC SCHOOLS RELIGION-STUDIES: 1975

BLUEPRINTS FOR THE FUTURE? MICHIGAN'S CERTIFICATION PROGRAMS
IN THE ACADEMIC STUDY OF RELIGIONS

Paul J. Will
Eastern Michigan University

Since the Supreme Court decision in the Abington vs. Schempp case
we have witnessed widening interest in the objective teaching about religion
in elementary and secondary schools throughout the United States. Various
innovative programs have resulted in new curricular materials. Yet, the
teacher remains the crucial factor in any successful instructional program.
An instructor without a basic knowledge of the world's religions and their
sacred writings, a sensitivity about the problem of objectivity in a
pluralistic society, and the ability to evaluate critically curricular
materials is severely handicapped for this undertaking. Without systematic
teacher training based on clear objectives and standards, plans for the
successful implementation of the academic study of religion will invariably
go aglimmering. Fortunately, an increasing number of professionals are
grappling with this thorny problem.[1]

To date, four states have approved religion per se as a certification
area.[2] The leader in this field both in terms of defined standards and number
of approved programs is the State of Michigan. Four institutions of higher
learning are approved for a five year provisional period to prepare teachers
for certification in the Academic Study of Religions. Calvin College was
approved in April 1972, Western Michigan University and Michigan State
University in January 1974, and Hope College in May 1975. In addition,
the applications of the University of Detroit, Alma College, Central
Michigan University, and Spring Arbor College await future action.

The initial impetus for the certification program in Michigan came
from Calvin College, a private four-year denominational college in the
western portion of the state. In 1967 an inquiry was made to the state
about the propriety of preparing teachers for certification in the area of
religion. In 1969 Calvin College formally requested the State Board of
Education to approve certification of a major and/or minor in "the history
and literature of religion." This request resulted in a study of
constitutional considerations, existing courses in Michigan schools, and
practices in other states. An advisory committee of professionals was
established to recommend a course of action to the State Board.[3]

The outcome of these deliberations was that in April 1970 the Michigan
State Board of Education approved the Academic Study of Religions as a minor
for elementary and secondary certification purposes. In addition to the
requirements for the minor, students have to complete those for education,
usually 24 to 32 hours, and a major of 30 hours. In the case of the
elementary curriculum three minors may be substituted for the major/minor
sequence. Usually the student selects a religion minor to complement an
English, history, or social studies major. Most distinct courses on religion
as well as units on religion are found in these departments in the public schools.

At the same time the Board approved the minor it adopted a set of standards which established a framework for evaluating institutional requests for approval. First, the college must be approved in three other certification areas to be eligible. It must show that the instructional staff have appropriate earned academic degrees, hold membership in learned societies, and make contributions to scholarly advancement through research. The program must be based on a comprehensive curriculum in the structure and history of religions. A rationale for the program must be provided. The relationship to other departments and professional educators, including plans for student teaching, must be defined. Finally, it must be shown that there are adequate library resources and instructional materials appropriate to the academic study of religions.[4]

To supplement these formal standards, a set of more specific program development suggestions was prepared by the advisory committee. These suggestions do not have official State Board approval. A number of specific recommendations are given in this document. There should be a systematic curriculum with required core offerings making up at least one-half of the proposed minor. All the major religions must be represented, including required offerings in Eastern religions. The need for an introductory course to provide a common orientation in methodology and ontology is emphasized. Consideration should be given to a course on the contemporary American religious situation. The inclusion of electives from related academic disciplines is encouraged. There also must be a program administrator, provision for a file of teaching materials, adequate budgetary support, and a system of program review.[5]

These two documents serve as practical guides for institutions preparing their proposals for review and State Board action. If the proposed program meets basic requirements regarding the form of the application it is submitted to a Committee of Scholars for review.[6] This committee is appointed by the State Board of Education. Its membership varies but has included professors of religion and education from both public and private colleges as well as representatives from the Michigan Department of Education. This committee reviews each proposal and makes recommendations. At least one visitation to the campus of the institution seeking approval is part of the committee's standard procedure.

In reviewing these proposals the committee has focused on a number of problems. A major concern in most cases is that the program components provide a balanced coverage of the major religious traditions and do not reflect a particular religious orientation. Usually schools are asked to clarify the relationship between the proposed program and the departmental committee structure of the school by including an organizational chart and program review procedures. The committee sees a need to assign responsibility for advising students and supervising directed teaching experiences. Formulation of a policy regarding the transfer of credit from other academic institutions is often another recommendation. Schools are questioned about the extent of teaching materials germane to the field that would be available to students.[7]

The Committee of Scholars is increasingly reluctant to recommend approval of a specific minor for elementary teachers in view of the need for broad, general preparation for the self-contained classroom situation. Apparently this attitude developed after the minor was initially adopted. The result is that Calvin College is approved for both elementary and secondary certification but the other programs are validated for the secondary level only.

Given these guidelines and suggestions there is still a fair amount of diversity in the programs approved by the State Board of Education. This leeway allows for the implementation of differing philosophies and techniques. A critical evaluation of the individual teacher-training curricula spotlights this divergence.

Calvin College had no initial model to refer to in creating its own program and this resulted in what, in some ways, is the most complex of the approved applications. A student is required to take 31.5 semester hours, significantly above the state minimum of 20 semester hours for a teaching minor. Although defined as an interdisciplinary group minor, the curriculum still relies heavily on Department of Religion offerings. Presently, six courses are required of all students: Introduction to Religion Studies, World Religions, Contemporary American Religious Situation, Historical and Theological Foundations of Religious Education, and two half courses, Readings and Research and Senior Seminar in Interpretation of Biblical Literature.[8]

Calvin is the only school so far to introduce changes in its program based on actual experience. The original proposal as approved in 1972 had a slightly different format. Before the final application was submitted to the state, Religion and Theology 205: World Religions was restructured and made a 300 level course. Then Philosophy/Religion 205 was created as Ethics (Religio-Ethical Systems) and was designed to:
> ...provide a methodology and ontology which are valid both descriptively and analytically for the academic study of several major world religions. The axiological structure of this required course also recognizes that the program of concentration to which it is an introduction is a teaching minor. Thus the axiological approach is appropriate because of its similarity and ready transfer to the study of religions in secondary and elementary schools where the prevailing motivation and context for such study is heavily oriented toward value education.[9]

This focus proved unmanageable and was replaced with one which includes methodology and stresses legal and curricular emphases. The course was renamed Introduction to Religion Studies. Religion 301 also underwent a transformation from Christianity and Culture, which covered the cultural impact of the religious traditions coming out of the Reformation, to the present Contemporary American Religious Situation. Interestingly, the Christianity and Culture course initially designated for use in the program was itself a modification of an earlier existing offering entitled Calvinism.

To further clarify the role of religion in education there is Historical and Theological Foundations of Religious Education, which "...is designed to give the student an understanding of how the various social institutions in society, such as home, church, school, government, etc. have organized themselves and their curriculum and teaching to meet their goals in a way consistent with existing religious values and within the legislative, judicial, and social limits placed upon each institution in various times, places, and religious traditions."[10] The half course in Reading and Research, an independent study-tutorial course, fills in any gaps left in the student's training especially in the areas of methods and professional attitude.

The remainder of the Calvin program involves four elective courses. Two courses must be taken from eleven offerings in Religion/Philosophy. These include theology, Biblical literature, and philosophy courses. Finally, two courses must be elected from three groups (History, English/Fine Arts, and Sociology/Psychology) each with four courses. No more than one selection may be made from any one group. The stated intent of this interdisciplinary requirement is to give students further exposure to non-Western religions.[11] A careful analysis of these offerings reveals that they barely touch on Asian religion, if at all, and have only a cursory religion component in general. The result is that most, and probably all, students would only have the one required general course in World Religions as their basis of knowledge about non-Western religions. This is clearly a weakness in the program.

I would also question the inclusion of theology courses in a minor in the academic study of religion approved by the state for the secular classroom. From a literal standpoint theology implies a sectarian view and while some courses under the rubric of theology have no denominational focus I believe that it is clearly advisable in constructing a minor of limited scope to exclude theological studies. Although I can conceive of situations where theological training could be utilized, its direct application and usefulness in the elementary and secondary settings is questionable. The State Board apparently does not share this concern, for the approved programs often contain such courses and the official standards state: "Religion as an academic discipline describes, interprets and compares sacred writings, creeds, theologies, mythologies, and cultic practices of a culture or cultures."[12] If theology is to be included in teacher preparation, a clearer definition of what this involves is needed. Nevertheless, it is difficult enough to convince educators in the public sector of the validity of teaching about religion without introducing such complications.

Elimination of both peripheral and purely theological courses from the list of electives would be an improvement. Clearly the major strength of the Calvin certification minor is the combination of a required core of over half the courses and an interdisciplinary component. There is evident concern with the appropriate methodology and attitude toward the subject matter. The willingness to change course content as the program evolves is laudable. The direction of this metamorphosis is in line with the unofficial program development suggestions distributed by the state.

In some respects, the plan of Western Michigan University's Department of Religion is the most intriguing. This 22 semester hour minor is based on the department's structure and its underlying philosophy that religion is an autonomous discipline with its own identifiable perspective and methodology. From the inception of the certification idea Western Michigan's faculty argued that this viewpoint should be the rationale for the teaching minor in Michigan. Even before any proposal gained approval they suggested particular criteria to the state for this new certification area. These were eloquently advocated and philosophically compelling in many ways.[13] While the State Board did not formally adopt Western Michigan's ideas in toto, some of their logic and even specific suggestions were incorporated into the official standards. For example, the requirements that an applying institution must be approved in at least three other certification areas and that instructors must hold academic rather than professional seminary degrees may be attributed to their influence.[14]

Western Michigan's approved program retains their original ideological perspective. Two courses of the six in the curriculum are required of all students: Introduction to Religion and The Teaching of Religion in the Public School. The latter two credit class represents a clear recognition of the special pedagogical problems in this field. Subsequent applications from other colleges to the state generally have adopted the idea that there should be a specific requirement in the methodology of teaching about religion in the elementary and secondary schools. The remainder of the minor provides for a series of choices within certain designated areas. A student is to select one course in primitive religions and one in the Christian, Jewish, or Islamic religious traditions within the departmental catagory of Historical Studies. One offering in Morphological and Phenomenological Studies is required. Finally, another course either in Historical Studies, other than those areas previously specified, or in Methodological Studies has to be elected.[15]

In my judgment, the absence of a required content course in Asian religions is a serious problem. Western Michigan's proposal recognized this lack but claimed knowledge about Eastern religions was implicit in its requirements.

Moreover, the rationale of the present proposal is such as to lead the student to investigate the nature and function of religion and the religious experience, or consciousness, as such. Consequently, the widest possible familiarity with religious phenomena is encouraged and heavy emphasis is placed on morphology and phenomenology both of which presuppose such broad familiarity.[16]

Despite the disclaimer, this is still a deficiency. Most teachers fail to have even a rudimentary understanding of the Asian traditions. Under Western Michigan's program a student can elect to avoid even a single offering on Eastern religions, although he is required to have a course on primitive religions.

It should be noted that the other disciplinary examinations of religion available under Methodological Studies are taught by religion department faculty and not professionals from those fields. However, the department has excluded from the certification options part of their regular curriculum entitled Constructive Studies, which includes courses on theology. Certainly, the experiences of those prepared by this unique program will be particularly valuable in determining the type of teacher-training model that is most viable.

Michigan State University's minor of 30 quarter hours, the equivalent of 20 semester hours, envisions a liberal elective system from the Department of Religious Studies' offerings. Three specific courses are required of all students: Understanding Religious Man, Introduction to Western Religions, and Introduction to Eastern Religions. Four elective courses must be taken in Western religions, with at least one in Judaic or Islamic studies. Three elective courses on Eastern religions complete the requirements.[17] The elective courses must be planned with the department's Teacher Certification Program Administrator. Under this scheme the student has the chance to concentrate on either textual or historical studies depending on his teaching goal, e.g. religious literature or history of religion. There are a number of theology courses available as departmental electives. The program has no methods course and no interdisciplinary offerings.

The strength of this curriculum is its balance between the Judeo-Christian and Asian traditions thereby insuring substantial coverage of the non-Western area. However, there is a disparity in available courses with twenty in Western religious traditions versus six in Asian religions, with two of these offered every other year. Moreover, this balance was achieved only after the Committee of Scholars recommended that the department revise its original plan. This first proposal, which was based on a slightly different departmental curriculum, called for two introductory courses, Introduction to Christianity and Comparative Religion, and nine credits in Biblical Studies. The student would select another nine credits from the field of either World Religions, Religion and Culture, Religious History, or Ethics and Theology. He would also take six credits of electives in the Department of Religion.[18]

The simplicity of the officially approved Michigan State program, with its stress on content offerings, raises the points of how specific and diversified the requirements should be for a teaching minor in religion. Some will argue that a minor is inadequate to the task and that a major concentration is needed. However, the State Board of Education has expressed its concern about the placement of these newly prepared teachers. Since it is unlikely that they will be teaching only courses dealing with religion, preparation in another academic area is essential. For the Michigan situation a minor accreditation seems to be the most practical. Thus the real issue for the present remains how many areas the minor can cover and how to delineate them in the curriculum.

The most recently approved collegiate application provides an interesting contrast to those previously mentioned. Hope College's minor appears to be the result of a careful analysis of the state's program suggestions and of a survey undertaken by Professor Lambert Ponstein in 1973. He found that the actual courses in religion offered in the high schools were almost equally divided between Bible as Literature and World Religions/Comparative Religions.[19] The Hope program therefore calls for an introductory course in the phenomenology of religion, two courses in the Western religious tradition, two sequential courses in Asian traditions, one interdisciplinary course, one course in Religion in America, and an education course entitled Teaching of Religion in Elementary and Secondary Schools. Provision is made for several possible course substitutions. Literature of Judaism and Christianity can be replaced by Religion in Society or Intertestamentary History. Religion and Psychology and Religion and Sociology can be substituted for Philosophy of Religion. Contemporary Religious Thought can take the place of Religion in America.[20]

The minor consists of 21 semester hours with the additional methods course of two hours. This program follows the advisory committee's guidelines more closely than any of the others. Given the credit hour limitations imposed by a certification minor, I feel that the Hope program does an admirable amount in terms of content coverage and methodology. Others may consider it too fragmented or rigid.

Curiously, all the efforts in creating these certification programs occurred almost simultaneously with a dramatic increase in courses offered in the secondary schools. Academicians did not have a clear picture of what was happening in the state until 1973 and apparently there is no causal correlation between these two events. The State Board of Education is still unaware of the extent of the actual teaching impact.

In 1975, twenty percent of the some 580 public senior high schools
in Michigan offer regular courses about religion or religious literature.
Many others include teaching units on religion in other courses. The 1973
Ponstein survey found 96 high schools with 104 distinct courses dealing with
religion. The results showed that most of these courses were introduced into
the school curriculum by enterprising educators since 1970.[21] A Fall 1974
study by Professor Henry Hoeks discovered an additional 19 senior high schools
teaching courses about religion. He found a growing number of junior high
schools offering units on religion.[22] No careful survey has been done on
the private school sector where there is increasing interest, especially
in comparative religion. This dramatic growth is not confined to any one
part of the state or type of school district.

During the last few years there has been a fair degree of cooperation
among academic professionals in the certification process and they have worked
together to reach career teachers already instructing about religion. This
mutual concern resulted in the creation of the Council on the Study of
Religion in Michigan Schools in March 1972. Fourteen institutions of
higher learning, both public and private, have joined the council and
provided a modest treasury. This has enabled the organization to sponsor
a survey of the Michigan public schools, prepare a bibliography of audio-visual
aids for teaching about religion, and publish a newsletter for educators
throughout the state. There are tentative plans to sponsor a state-wide
awareness conference to faciliatate a continuing discussion about methodology
and curricular materials.[23]

Various colleges also have taken individual initiative. A number have
held one-day institutes during the past years. In the summer of 1975 credit
courses in the academic study of religion specificially designed for teachers
were offered by the University of Detroit and Central Michigan University.
Western Michigan University launched a new Master of Arts in the Teaching
of the Academic Study of Religions in Fall 1975. It represents an effort
to reach mid-career public school teachers and others interested in teaching
about religion with appropriate professional training.[24] It is unclear
whether such graduate programs will be considered by the state as qualifying
for certification in the academic study of religions.

There are a number of other unanswered questions. What would the
repercussions be if the state required those already teaching courses to
have minor certification in the academic study of religions? There are over
150 instructors with virtually no formal training presently teaching. Only
a limited number of undergraduate students, an average of 10-20 per
institution, are enrolled in the approved programs. Could a truly interdisciplinary proposal rather than a departmental application gain approval?
So far only departments of religion have filed applications. Will the state
grant final approval to these programs after the five year provisional period
has expired? Presently annual statements reporting program developments
must be filed with the state by the schools.

The State of Michigan has thus established general standards but
no rigid criteria for the undergraduate certification minor. The more
specific program component suggestions are not literally adhered to and
remain unofficial. All approved colleges include an introductory course
for orientation in the discipline of religion and the religious dimension
in human experience. This is also true of the pending programs of the

University of Detroit and Central Michigan University.[25] However, this
is the only suggested course subscribed to by all schools. Only the
private colleges meet the recommendation of having at least one-half
of the courses required of all candidates. Apparently, there is little
interest in including courses from related disciplines. Most schools
have a course on Religion in America available.

The inclusion of courses on Eastern religions as required core
offerings is often ignored or minimized. Philosophic polemics temporarily
aside, one could argue for their adoption on mere pragmatic grounds, for
half of the courses taught in Michigan public high schools are in world
religions. On the other hand, such a rationale itself inevitably raises
a philosophical question. Should Asian religions be required in the
certification minor not on the basis of comprehensiveness but because of
its usefulness in the actual classroom situation? If so, then the same logic
would justify requiring a course on Bible as Literature, etc.[26] The question
is ultimately whether the high school curricular offerings should dictate
the form of the teacher preparation program. Or should the colleges concentrate
on preparing teachers in a theoretical and methodological understanding of
religion and its role in human culture and let high school courses evolve out
of this context? No consensus regarding this problem has emerged among
professionals in religion and education, nor is one likely soon.

A pre-eminent question is to what extent these programs are useful
not only for teacher preparation now but as models for future developments.
Has the state been too lax or too restrictive? Or has it struck the golden
mean that allows for a fair degree of experimentation within a sound academic
and pedagogical framework? Perhaps the major contribution of the Michigan
certification programs is in providing a variety of actual curricular models
rather than abstract theoretical structures that can be analyzed. The
teachers produced by these programs and their experiences in the schools
may provide the final verdict on their value.

Footnotes

[1]For example, see Frank L. Steeves, <u>State-Approved Curricula in Religious Studies</u>, September 15, 1973 (Public Education Religion Studies Center Reprint) and E. Richard Barnes, Joseph Forcinelli, Alpha Montgomery, <u>A Proposal for Single Subject Credential Additions in the Academic Study about Religion,</u> <u>Submitted to the California State Board of Education Upon the Recommendation</u> <u>of the Subcommittee on Credentialing in Teaching about Religion</u>, December 1972.

[2]Besides Michigan's certification programs in religion, there is Wisconsin with three (University of Wisconsin-Whitewater, Edgewood College, and Marquette University), California with two (University of California-Santa Barbara and California State University-Northridge), and Vermont with one (University of Vermont). The California situation is unclear due to a recent reordering of certification and licensing standards. Other states like Colorado, Maryland, Texas, and Iowa, are considering certification in this area. A 1969 <u>Survey</u> <u>of Certification Practices with Regard to Religion in the Fifty States</u> conducted by the Michigan Department of Education found only 24 of 44 responding states had consistently negative reactions to four questions concerning the appropriateness of religion as a teaching area.

[3]Department of Education, State of Michigan, <u>Preparing Teachers for the</u> <u>Academic Study of Religions</u>, September 30, 1970.

[4]Department of Education, State of Michigan, <u>Standards for Approval</u> <u>of The Academic Study of Religions for the Certification of Teachers</u>, n.d.

[5]Department of Education, State of Michigan, <u>Program Development</u> <u>Suggestions for Teaching Minor in the Academic Study of Religions</u>, n.d.

[6]Usually the application is filed using the official form, <u>Request</u> <u>for State Board Approval Amended or New Teacher Education Program</u>, available from Teacher Education and Certification Division, Bureau of Higher Education, Department of Education, State of Michigan.

[7]As seen in Department of Education, State of Michigan, <u>Report of Committee</u> <u>of Scholars Regarding Michigan State University Request for Approval of a</u> <u>Teaching Minor in the Academic Study of Religion</u>, November 30, 1972; <u>Report of</u> <u>Committee of Scholars Regarding Western Michigan University Request for Approval</u> <u>of a Teaching Minor in the Academic Study of Religions</u>, November 30, 1972; and <u>Report of Committee of Scholars Regarding Hope College Request for Approval</u> <u>of a Teaching Minor in the Academic Study of Religions</u>, n.d.

[8]<u>Request of Calvin College to the State of Michigan Department of Education</u> <u>to Add the Academic Study of Religions as a Certifiable Teaching Minor in its</u> <u>Secondary and Elementary Teacher Education Programs</u>, October 20, 1971.

[9]<u>Ibid.</u>, p. 11.

[10]<u>Ibid.</u>, p. 12.

[11]<u>Ibid.</u>, p. 13.

[12]Department of Education, State of Michigan, <u>Standards for Approval</u> <u>of The Academic Study of Religions for the Certification of Teachers</u>, n.d.

102

Department of Religion, Western Michigan University, Suggested Criteria for the Training of Public School Teachers in the Discipline of the Academic Study of Religions, (Revised as of September, 1970) and Guntram G. Bischoff, "Toward the Academic Study of Religions in the Public School? Reflections Occasioned by Recent Developments in Michigan" in the Bulletin of the Council on the Study of Religion, vol. 2, no. 2 (April 1971), p. 3-10.

[14]Minutes of Meeting of the Committee on Religious Education, Bureau of Higher Education, Michigan Department of Education, February 19, 1970. Their recommendations were adopted by the State Board of Education in April 1970.

[15]Department of Religion, Western Michigan University, Request for State Board Approval of an Amended or New Teacher Education Program, n.d.

[16]Department of Religion, Western Michigan University, Response to the Document, "Program Development Suggestions for Teaching Minor in the Academic Study of Religions," issued by Department of Education, State of Michigan, and received at the Department of Religion, Western Michigan University on April 24, 1972, n.d.

[17]Department of Religious Studies, Michigan State University, Request for Authorization to Offer a Teaching Minor in the Academic Study of Religions, n.d.

[18]Department of Religion, Michigan State University, Request for Authorization to Offer a Teaching Minor in Religion, n.d.

[19]Untitled summary of the survey on the teaching of world religions in the public schools of Michigan, October 12, 1973. The results showed 104 courses distributed as follows: World Religions - 22, Comparative Religions - 22, The Bible as Literature - 42, History of Religion - 6, Great Western Religions - 1, Bible History, Old Testament - 3, Bible History, New Testament - 3, Humanities, Discussion of Religions and Religious Beliefs - 3, Religion in America - 1, and History of the Bible - 1.

[20]Request of Hope College to the State of Michigan Department of Education for the Purpose of Adding the Academic Study of Religions as a Certifiable Minor in its Elementary and Secondary Teacher Education Programs, January 31, 1973.

[21]Lambert Ponstein, untitled summary of the survey on the teaching of world religions in the public schools of Michigan, October 12, 1973. Of the 77 schools that indicated the year the course(s) were started the distribution was: 1960 and before - 2, 1961 - 1, 1962 - 1, 1964 - 3, 1968 - 6, 1969 - 5, 1970 - 14, 1971 - 15, 1972 - 20, and 1973 (partial) - 10.

[22]Untitled summary of responses to an initial questionnaire in the survey of the academic teaching and study of religions in the secondary (7-12) schools in Michigan, sponsored by the Council on the Study of Religion in Michigan Schools, n.d.

[23]Paul J. Will, "Teacher Certification: Michigan's Approach to Teaching about Religion," in Religion and Public Education, ed. David E. Engel, (Paramus, N.J., Paulist Press, 1974), p. 162-163.

[24]Department of Religion, Western Michigan University, Proposal for a Master of Arts in the Teaching of the Academic Study of Religions Degree Program, n.d.

[25]Department of Religious Studies, University of Detroit, Request for State Board Approval of Teacher Education Program Changes, September 26, 1974 and Department of Religion, Central Michigan University, The Teaching Minor in the Academic Study of Religion; Central Michigan University; A Guide for Prospective Students; Subject to Approval by Michigan State Department of Education, n.d.

[26]The use of the designation "Bible as Literature" is often an inaccurate euphemism. How can one remove the metaphysical content from the Bible and only view it as a mere compendium of literary genres? I find the title used in Pennsylvania, "Religious Literature of the West," more representative and useful.

RELIGION IN HUMAN CULTURE:
THE DEVELOPMENT OF A
MODEL COURSE IN WORLD RELIGIONS

Lee Smith
Project Director

Wes Bodin
Program Director

World Religions Curriculum Development Center
Minneapolis, MN 55426

Religion in Human Culture is a course designed for high schools that choose to
teach about religion. It is a social studies course about religion designed
to enhance human dignity and utilize rational processes in its learning activities. It is a course which helps students learn about the religious diversity of the world, to develop attitudes of understanding and respect for the
beliefs and practices of others and the legitimacy of those beliefs and
practices in a world of pluralism and mobility consistent with the 1963
U.S. Supreme Court Schempp Decision which holds that schools shall neither
practice nor profess any religion, but should teach about religions.

The developmental process involves student and community advisory committees,
professional consultants from the academic study of religion, the social
sciences, history and curriculum development. The process also involves
three successive rounds of field testing with youngsters to determine "what
works" and "what has integrity," followed by a revision process based on field
test data and sponsorship of in-service teacher-training workshops, to
facilitate the implementation of the course, the field testing and revision
processes. Comprehensive evaluation and monitoring is conducted by Guardian
Resource Development, Inc., an independent contractor.

COURSE OUTLINE

Part I. Building a Model for Learning about the Diversity of Religions

         Unit A. Religious Expression in Human Culture
              B. The Function of Religion in Human Culture
              C. Perceiving and Understanding Religious Expression

Part II. Exploring Selected Religious Traditions-Application of the Model

         Unit A. Hinduism   E. Islam   I. Jainism
              B. Buddhism   F. Taoism   J. Zoroastrianism
              C. Judaism   G. Sikhism   K. Shinto
              D. Christianity H. Confucianism

105

Part III.   Independent Study and Field Work

An application of the model through the pursuit of individual and small group interest in specific religions, religious issues or topics.

Part IV.   Religious Issues in Contemporary Culture

Unit A.   Religion and Culture Change
     B.   Religion and Public Policy

COURSE OBJECTIVES

Introduction

The course objectives for Religion in Human Culture lie within the four categories established by the National Council for the Social Studies Curriculum Guidelines (1971). The categories are:

  I.   Knowledge
 II.   Abilities
III.   Valuing
 IV.   Social Participation

Because Religion in Human Culture is conceived as a social studies course, an attempt has been made to keep its pattern of development consistent with the rationale of the Social Studies Curriculum Guidelines. However, while the developers seek to pursue the processes of rational and objective inquiry, they also make a serious effort to maintain the imprecise, delicate and very human qualities that religion represents. As one of the project's consultants, Dr. Thomas Kraabel, put it: "in an attempt to be scientific, one must take care to do a physical and mental examination rather than an autopsy."

The user of this course should keep the following cautions in mind with regard to the course objectives:

1.   The course objectives are general, broad statements whose purposes are to control the direction of the course. Therefore, the instructional objectives, learning materials and teaching procedures are designed to ultimately cause students to grow and develop in terms of the stated course objectives.

2.   Conceptual knowledge, enhanced abilities, attitudes and values are not conceived to be fixed categories that can be attained and precisely measured. They are, in fact, open categories which can continue to grow and develop throughout life. In essence, they are much like the knowledge of music and the skills possessed by a piano player - growth, improvement, and maturity, while entirely noticeable, may never be fully realized. Many of the concepts, abilities, attitudes and values in this course will have been long established in good programs prior to coming to this course, and although the objectives are not developed sequentially in this course there is a building process involved. The teacher should not despair because dramatic

changes do not appear with each lesson. Because the objectives re-occur throughout the course, the students progress can be likened to that of the piano student - practice provides growth and development.

3. Most of the objectives do not "break out" in "clean" categories. There is a constant interplay between knowledge, abilities, attitudes and values and participation in the societal life of the "real world." Content and process are inseparable except for purposes of academic analysis.

4. The teacher is urged to consult the chart which keys the individual lessons to the "course objective" on a regular basis, and to note carefully that the instructional objectives for each lesson are keyed to the course objectives.

5. The course objectives were designed to provide over-all direction for the course. The teacher must take care to keep them in mind throughout the entire course. It is probable that all course objectives could be stated for nearly all lessons. The course objectives are implicit in most lessons.

6. The Instructional Objectives, specified in each lesson, serve to focus attention on the specific emphasis of each lesson. Ultimately the instructional objectives contribute to the attainment of the course objectives.

Course Objectives

I. Knowledge Objectives

A. Religious Diversity

Upon completion of the course students will be able to demonstrate, by specific examples, illustrations and explanations, a knowledge of religious diversity and the diversity of religious expression.

1. Further, students will demonstrate that religious diversity is normal and legitimate.
2. Further, students will demonstrate a knowledge of factors which cause or contribute to religious diversity.
3. Further, students will demonstrate a knowledge of the complexity of religious diversity.

B. Functions of Religion

Upon completion of the course students will be able to demonstrate, by specific examples, illustrations and explanations a knowledge of the functions of religion.

1. Further, students will demonstrate a knowledge of certain "universal" functions of religions.
2. Further, students will demonstrate a knowledge of certain "unique" functions of specific religions.

C. Continuity and Change

Upon completion of the course students will demonstrate, by specific
examples, illustrations, and explanations, a knowledge of the concepts of continuity and change as they relate to religious phenomena.

1. Further, students will demonstrate a knowledge of how
    historical experience shapes religion.
2. Further, students will demonstrate a knowledge of how religion
    shapes historical experience.
3. Further, students will demonstrate a knowledge of the factors
    which cause and inhibit change.

D. Stereotypes

Upon completion of the course students will be able to demonstrate,
by specific examples, illustrations and explanations, a knowledge of
religious stereotypes and their effects.

E. Religious Expression

Upon completion of the course students will demonstrate, by specific
examples, illustrations and explanations, a knowledge of religious
expression.

1. Further, students will demonstrate a knowledge of the diversity
    of religious expression.
2. Further, students will demonstrate a knowledge of the problems
    of interpreting and attaching meaning to various forms of
    religious expression.
3. Further, students will demonstrate a knowledge of causes and
    sources of motivation giving rise to certain specific
    expressions of religion.
4. Further, students will demonstrate a knowledge that religious
    expression provides a data base for studying about religion.

F. Conflict and Conflict Resolution

Upon completion of the course students will demonstrate, by specific
examples, illustrations and explanations, a knowledge of the nature
of conflict, its causes and effects, and conflict resolution as they
relate to religion.

II. Ability and Skill Objectives

A. Awareness and Perception Abilities

Upon completion of the course students will have demonstrated the
ability to perceive religious phenomena by utilizing the skills
of observation, formulation of questions, formulation of hypothesis,
and formulation of definitions.

B. Information Gathering Abilities

   Upon completion of the course students will have demonstrated the
   ability to gather information by utilizing skills of locating,
   listening, reading, interviewing, and participant observation.

C. Information Processing Abilities

   Upon completion of the course students will have demonstrated the
   ability to process information by utilizing the skills of organization
   and classification, analysis (checking bias, objectivity, appropriateness), synthesis and evaluation.

D. Information Utilization and Application Abilities

   Upon completion of the course students will have demonstrated the
   ability to utilize and apply information by employing the skills of
   generalizing, speaking, writing, presenting and problem solving.

E. Effective Participation Abilities

   Upon completion of the course students will have demonstrated the
   ability to participate effectively by utilizing skills of active
   listening, sharing, cooperation and leadership.

III. Attitudes and Values Objectives

   A. Curiosity

      Upon completion of the course students will have demonstrated an
      attitude of curiosity toward their own religious ideas and practices
      and those of others by their willingness to ask questions, to listen,
      and to learn about their own and the religious ideas, traditions and
      practices of others.

   B. Objectivity

      Upon completion of the course students will have demonstrated a value
      of objectivity toward religious beliefs, practices, and information by
      skepticism, tolerance for ambiguity, willingness to suspend judgment,
      respect for the use of reason and respect for the quantity and quality
      of evidence as a test for accuracy.

   C. Respect

      Upon completion of the course students will have demonstrated an
      attitude of respect for the religious ideas and practices of others
      based on the value of human dignity and the value of the right to
      individual choice.

IV. Social Participation Objective

Upon completion of the course, students will be able to demonstrate an <u>ability to participate effectively in society</u> by dealing with people as individuals rather than categories, by using their abilities and knowledge in working toward the solution of problems related to religion which effect individuals and groups in society and in the world.

Public Education Religion Studies: Toward An Operational
Process Methodology For Science, Religion and Ethics

Barbara Ann Swyhart, Ph.D.
Assistant Professor
Coordinator, Religion and Public Education
San Diego State University

While much is being discussed and written in the areas of World Religion, and
Religion in America, in public education, little attention is given to the
problematic of a methodology for religion studies in the areas which involve
ethical and scientific problems, both individual and social. Values clarification
as a method of instruction enables students to surface the assumptions and
implicit values within their own and others' thought and action patterns.
However, this method does not delve into the problematic of the process of
decision-making which implicitly follows the methodology of paradigmatic events
and/or models. I propose to explain the way in which a modified operational
approach, i.e. Paradigms-of-Reality-in-Process, may provide a viable methodology
for the teaching of religion maintaining four important criteria: 1) respect for
plural religious forms; 2) the integrity of the unity of each model in and by
itself; 3) the health of the student in an organic approach to the perception of
viable, yet often conflicting and/or paradoxical issues; 4) the realization of
concrete realities of individual and social significance toward the process of
decision making in a technological and scientific environment. The Plover Book
series will be used as illustrative of the goals mentioned. I will offer
suggestions for the use of the process expressed in this series within a religious
context. This perspective inaugurates a mean between method as technique and
methodology as the formal vehicle in which distinctions such as functional
vs. substantive may be adequately maintained and used in the context of the
paradigm presented.

        In a recent issue of the Journal For The Scientific Study of Religion,
sociologist Peter L. Berger reemphasized a critical distinction between the
actual operability of the two leading contenders in the controversial inquiry
into the methodology for the scientific study of religion i.e., "substantive"
versus "functional" definitions of religion.[1] Acknowledging that definitions
"are always ad hoc constructs," [2] Professor Berger suggests that religion
defined substantively, that is "in terms of the meaning contents of the phenomenon," and, religion defined functionally, that is "in terms of its place
in the social and/or psychological system,"[3] do not meet the need for the
maintenance of the transcendent quality which religion is about. Instead he
offers a phenomenology of religion "from within" based on Alfred Schutz' analysis
of the "multiple realities" of human experience[4]. Coupling the world of
"paramount reality," ("the everyday 'life-world'"; "the taken-for-granted world
of commonsense"),[5] with its contents (the "finite provinces of meanings"),
religion is seen as potentially mediated by both of these boundaries and thus
bi-polar in its structure. Seen as having multiple dimensions "paramount realities"
contain the thrust of the religious perspective. While this methodology is
an "epistemologically neutral . . . enterprise" it is also, "methodologically
atheistic."[6]

        I have chosen to approach my subject by re-acquainting the reader with
this methodological issue, so well expressed in Professor Berger's article, for
two reasons. First, it openly confesses the possibilities and limits of the
three approaches described above, as well as expressing the most important
current methodologies for adaptation in a high school classroom; second,

112

Professor Berger's argument will be useful to offset and contrast what I
propose as a modified operationalism, i.e., Paradigms-of-Reality-In-Process, in
part based on Professor P.W. Bridgman's description of "the operational point of
view," i.e., "in that we shall no longer permit ourselves to use as tools in our
thinking concepts of which we cannot give an adequate account in terms of
operation."[7] Paradigms-of-Reality-In-Process is therefore concerned with the
reconstruction of conceptual tools for reflection on problems with a distinct,
yet relational, focus.

I would propose at the outset that three issues must be addressed: 1)
the special nature of a "problems" approach to religion studies, particularly in
the areas of science and religion, and, ethics and religion; 2) the advisability
of an epistemologically neutral methodology, although not equating this with
"methodological atheism; 3) the nature of "paradigms-of-reality-in-process as a
construct based on three forms of thought: a) operationalism, b) Thoman Kuhn's
ethic and psychology of Alfred North Whitehead.[8]

In approaching a course in world religions, curriculum materials while
not innumerable, offer, more often than not, a substantive approach to the
nature of religious traditions. Within the public school parameters any approach
that is "experience oriented" is suspect and usually very difficult to balance
on the bars of religious pluralism. Further, the functional approach which
tends "to be used" rather than illustrative of religious awareness in a
multi-disciplinary vein, is equally suspect. If subjectivity is misunderstood
"the tacit dimension" [9] is feared as a bias rather than a natural, existential
condition of human communication. At the high school level we cannot afford to
choose either methodology due to the delicate nature of what is to be communicated.
It is equally misleading to present religions as if they were simply a bubble
transparent to the world of "permanent realities," but not of, or in, the world
itself. Within the realm of teaching about the confrontation of another discipline
with religion, specifically science and/or ethics, the neutral character of the
methodology must be invested with the keen sensitivity and sharp acumen of the
instructor. This demands a different pedagogical character. A set of operable
paradigms historically and thematically ordered, as well as a comparative
religious interweave which maintains the integrity of the discipline of religion,
could present a fourth methodology for the study of religion in this problematic
focus.

Although the phenomenology of Alfred Schutz may be adequate to the
task of a phenomenology of world religions, it is difficult to demand the same
"withinness" in individual and social moral dilemmas which of necessity must be
described from multiple points of view, or, in the meeting of science and
religion which bears an indubitable historical truth stamp. In spite of "the
experiential and the "world of the every-day" historical truth overshadows the
good will of individuals and the noble ethical ideals of religious traditions.
This is the problem and the paradox. Multiple levels of truth and consequently
multiple levels of discourse do in fact grasp each truth distinctly and often
contrastingly. Within a modified operational methodology the language of
absolute vs. relative, descriptive vs. normative etc. are modified and the term
"construct" may be used in conjunction with the paradigm studied.

A construct is described by Professor P.W. Bridgman as consisting of
1) a unique correlation between a corresponding set of operations (i.e. concept)
and the physical data in terms of which it is defined; 2) a connection with
other physical phenomena independent of those which entered into its definition.[10] For example, "God," "justice,"[9] "love" may be approached as constructs
operating out of a specific paradigm (Judaism, Hinduism, etc.) to create a
reality-in-process, i.e., in relation to the individual, the social and the
personal.

> The use of the term "construct" in ethical discourse suggests
> that the method whereby decisions are made has confronted
> a) the hard data drawn from the discipline or study to which
> the decision will refer; b) the meeting of ontological priorities,
> i.e., the individual must meet the reality of the society through
> the personal while the society must not suppress the reality of
> the individual as personal. The operational perspective, then,
> contrary to strict Skinner behaviorism, creates a free-flowing
> interchange of data, ideas, and methods with the constructs it
> utilizes toward a process of decision-making.

In relating to this paradox a modified operationalism coupled with
process thought is helpful. A neutral epistemology must lay out its own language
and set up its structures of procedure. Three safeguards prevent it from
disintegrating into a merely subjective approach: a) historical realism; b)
comparative analysis; c) process itself as outlined by Alfred North Whitehead.
Neutrality must be the goal, although within any given discussion the experiential
and emotive factors are likely to be loud and clear. Laboring under the belief
that men and women operate scientifically and ethically from an implicit and
explicit set of assumptions about their world one can assume that paradigms can
be described given the constraints of each paradigm and the attendant possible
limitations and developments. Perhaps this bears the ring of values clarification[12]
and indeed to some extent it does. However, the difference is that values
operate by virtue of different paradigms, and causuistric "what if" situations
are not sufficient to demonstrate the actualities. Games[13] are replaced by actualities in
process with multi-dimensional paradoxes.

Ian Barbour, in _Myths, Models and Paradigms_,[14] discloses the nature of
a "model" as derived from science and technology. The adapted definition is
applied to the problematic of Jewish and Christian "models" of thought and
behavior. I prefer the use of Thomas Kuhn's definition of paradigm, which
closely parallels Barbour's definition of model minus one flaw. Models suggest
"perfected examples" to our ordinary understanding instead of pictures or images
from which to recreate one's own reality. Kuhn defines paradigms as,

> universally recognized scientific achievements that
> for a time provide model problems and solutions to a
> community of practitioners.[15]

In the methodology, paradigms-of-reality-in-process, "religious" may be substituted for "scientific". On the other hand, Barbour defines a model as,

> a symbolic representation of selected aspects of the
> behavior of a complex system for particular purposes.
> It is an imaginative tool for ordering experience, rather
> than a description of the world.[16]

He uses "paradigm" only as,

a tradition transmitted through historical examples.[17]

Models, however, if defined carefully, could be operable for the high school class. Yet, if paradigm could be well used, then I suggest preference for it since it would not have the "ordinary usage" taboo which would quickly abuse its intention.

The last aspect of this methodology involves the organic inter-relationship of multiple levels of existence expressed through process thought. Since we are not relating to religion in a static way, it is necessary that religion be set in context. Whitehead states:

> Religion is the vision of something which stands beyond, behind and within, the passing flux of immediate things; something which is real, and yet waiting to be realized; something which is a remote possibility, and yet the greatest of present facts; something that gives meaning to all that passes, and yet eludes apprehension; something whose possession is the final good, and yet is beyond all reach; something which is the ultimate ideal, and the hopeless quest.[18]

Religion provides an expression of "character," a complex of value experiences which give a sense of unity to one's life. It is a process of "making important" that must be taught instead of "what" is important.[19] For, I believe, that the "what" changes rapidly and who, not what, religion develops is the person able to see within and without the complexities of human and cosmic reality. Within the parameters of ontology, a process methodology for a problematic study of religion is able to freely move allowing the decision-making process the place of importance.

The Plover Book series,[20] which I have examined, is one that is sufficiently epistemologically neutral and could elicit the response of various paradigms in understanding the multi-dimensionality of its issues.[21] Further, the divergent methodologies i.e., functional, substantive, multi-dimensional, and paradigms-of-reality-in-process, may be live options for the context of the ethical problematic. The series is process oriented. Ideally, however, the future will bring texts specifically designed for a comparative religion-issue oriented perspective. As a start this series could provide a basis for a curriculum structure through both of these concerns. One example is provided in the following excerpt from <u>Deciding How To Live As Society's Children</u>.

> Rather than be drafted, Abraham's son, Joseph, went to Canada. He was sincerely convinced that the Thieu regime in South Vietnam was a corrupt dictatorship and that the whole American involvement in the war was a serious mistake. Now that the war is over, he cannot return home without being imprisoned for draft evasion. Abraham is bewildered by his son's behavior. To Abraham, his son is a coward--someone who ran out on his duty.
>
> Abraham fought bravely for the Allied Forces in World War II. Each day, he faced the possibility of death, but his fear was tempered by the conviction that he was fighting to protect his wife and family from the Nazi menace. Abraham feels that when he enlisted he was really only a boy.

> When he completed his tour of duty, he returned home a
> man. He had learned self-discipline, courage, and the
> manly art of self-defense.
>
> Abraham argues that military service is just what the
> young men in our country need to become mature.
>
> How do Abraham and his son perceive the different wars
> in which they are asked to participate? What does
> society say is the expected way to act?
>
> Do you agree with the father that Joe is a coward? Justify
> your statement. What price does Joseph pay for living out
> his convictions?[22]

Instead of the values' questions being raised, alternate religious paradigms such as the Bhagavad Gita and Confucianism could be discussed, each having its own particular set of constructs.

One of the problems in California, in connection with the guidelines for the teaching about religion, concerns teaching about morality and the teaching about religion. Both have been subsumed within the same set of guidelines and have often been confused. I believe, however, and have endeavored to develop the Pilot Project on this premise, the difference between teaching about morality and teaching about religion: they must remain distinct. It is in the area of teaching about religious values that the ethician would function in one role, that of the elementary and secondary school levels.

I have introduced in my Religious Ethics and Medical Problems course a discussion of the role of the "ethician" in a composite image of the medical setting, the educational setting and in the continuing education setting for professionals. Public and private education could contribute to the redefinition of a much needed resource--an ethician within the community of concern the medical profession and its attendant problems create. This term is a morally neutral term. I would, for example, see the work of Daniel Callahan, on the one hand, and Paul Ramsey on the other, creating the difference between the ethician and the moral theologian. This same distinction would apply to the role of the ethician in a public setting as opposed to the moral theologian in the private or parochial setting. I would stretch the analogy to include the academic teaching about religion vis a vis religious study and/or theology.

In the matter of science and religion, a similar methodology could be employed, this time the focus would be the paradigms of science and the meeting and/or mismeeting of religion. To enliven a historical perspective, various religious paradigms could be discussed as alternative responses to historical events and theories, for example the relation among the principles of theoretical physics, Buddhism and Whitehead, or atomism--Buddhist, Greek and Newtonian.

The above methodology must be set in a public school curriculum, a curriculum which legally and justly requires a commitment to religion studies which I describe as "detached academic enthusiasm and appreciation." In a previous paper delivered to the American Academy of Religion,[20] I spoke about our project in San Diego as well as the academic criteria for a teacher education program. This year two developments may be shared: 1) the establishment of a Religious Studies emphasis within the Social Science Teaching Credential; 2) an In-Service course for teachers in the city and county districts of San Diego.

While the last is in process at the writing of this paper, I do envision the
difficulty of informing students of problem areas as I have described, without
the neutral language of constructs and a modified operationalism in a process
defined "in relation to . . . ." However, in pursuing a viable methodology of
the problematic of science and religion and/or ethics and religion, creative and
yet structured energy must be expended to educate students and teachers of
religion. The category of religious educator must be transcended. This requires
a keen sensibility to the life of a religion while at the same time assuming that
a faith stance in the religion under discussion is not necessary. I see religion
in the broadest dimension of the ethical derived from the meeting of science
and religion. As such, respect for each tradition and the concerns of each
tradition represent a funnel for an overriding concern--that religion be taught
because of its essential qualitative contribution to civilizational advancement
as well as, unfortunately, to civilizational entrophy.

Footnotes

[1] Peter L. Berger, "Some Second Thoughts on Substantive versus Functional Definitions of Religion," Journal For The Scientific Study of Religion XIII, #2, 1974, pp. 125-133.

[2] Ibid., p. 127

[3] Ibid., p. 126

[4] Ibid., p. 129

[5] Ibid., p. 129

[6] Ibid., p. 133

[7] I am employing the operational language of P.W. Bridgman in The Logic of Modern Physics, (N.Y.: Macmillan, 1927), p. 31; cf. p. 7, "The true meaning of a term is to be found by observing what a man does with it, not by what he says about it." cf. P.W. Bridgman, The Intelligent Individual and Society, (N.Y.: Macmillan, 1938), p. 20. Operational analysis is described as what one is doing in using a term or answering a question.

[8] As suggested in Swyhart, Bioethics and Decision-making: Releasing Religion from the Spiritual, Chapter III, "Alfred North Whitehead on 'Importance' and 'Value,' to be published by Fortress Press, Fall-Winter, 1975.

[9] cf. Michael Polanyi, The Tacit Dimension, (Garden City: N.Y.: Doubleday (Anchor), 1966); and, Personal Knowledge: Toward a Post-Critical Philosophy, (New York: Harper Torchbooks, 1964); Harry Prosch, "Cooling The Modern Mind: Polanyi's Mission," Skidmore College Bulletin LVI, #4, August, 1971, p. 14. A Skidmore College Faculty Research Lecture, 1971.

[10] Bridgman, op. cit., pp. 53; 55-56.

[11] Swyhart, op. cit., ms. p. 19.

[12] Sidney B. Simon, Leland W. Howe, Howard Kirschenbaum, Values Clarification: A Handbook of Practical Strategies For Teachers and Students, (N.Y.: Hart Pub. Co., 1972); Sidney B. Simon, Lewis E. Raths, Merill Harmin, Values and Teaching, (Columbus: Charles E. Merrill and Company, 1966). Cf. Michael Donnellan, "Religion and Value Education," National Council on Religion and Public Education, II, #1, February, 1975, p. 2.

[13] cf. Virginia Buus and George McFarland, "Simulation Gaming and Religious Education," A Special Theme Section in Simulation/Gaming/News, March 1974, pp. 6-13.

[14] Ian G. Barbour, Myths, Models and Paradigms, (N.Y.: Harper and Row, 1974); cf. Ian G. Barbour, Science and Secularity, (N.Y.: Harper and Row, 1970).

[15] Thomas S. Kuhn, The Structure of Scientific Revolutions, 2nd ed., enlarged, (Chicago: University of Chicago Press, 1927), p. viii.

[16] Barbour, Myths, Models and Paradigms, op. cit., p.6.

118

[17] Ibid., p.9.

[18] Alfred North Whitehead, _Science and the Modern World_, (N.Y.: Macmillan, 1953 (1925)), pp. 191-192.

[19] cf. Swyhart, _op. cit_, ms. p. 72.

[20] cf. Rodney F. Allen, _Teaching Guide For the Plover Books_ (Terrace Heights, Winona, Mass: St. Marys' College Press (Plover Books), 1974); Sheila O'Fahey, Pamela Cary Betz, Frances Gelsone, Ronald W. Petrich, _Deciding How To Live as Society's Children_: Individual Needs and Institutional Expectations, (Winona: St. Mary's College Press (Plover Books), 1974), and, Maureen Carey, Paul Chapman, Robert Cunnane, Antony Mullaney, Anne Walsh, _Deciding on The Human Use of Power_: The Exercise and Control of Power in an Age of Crisis, (Winona: St. Mary's College Press (Plover Books), 1974).

[21] cf. _Deciding On The Human Use of Power_, op. cit. pp. 33-56.

[22] _Deciding How To Live as Society's Children_, op. cit, p. 30.

THE PROBLEM OF NORM IN PUBLIC EDUCATION RELIGION STUDIES:

ENLIGHTENMENT, EMANCIPATION OR SOCIALIZATION

by

John R. Whitney

Virginia Theological Seminary

In accepting this assignment the author takes seriously the significance of the three designated terms we are to relate to the normative problem in religion studies in the public schools, viz., enlightenment, which I see connoting worship and learning; socialization, connoting social order and industry; and emancipation, connoting individual and group freedom. I prefer to arrange them seriatim this way rather than as they are ordered in the title since I believe this is the more typical sequence in which we encounter them as developmental processes in our personal experience. In real life emancipation depends on a prior socialization and socialization depends on a prior enlightenment. This triadic process of course is a cumulative one in that first enlightenment must begin and continue, then socialization must begin and continue, and finally emancipation must begin and continue along with the other two. The first enables the second, the first and second enable the third. Perhaps the sequence is more easily seen this way in reason than in practice. Nevertheless I believe the priorities to be functional in most healthy human development, both in the family and in the larger more public society.

Let me comment on the problem of norm. In this paper the treatment of norm will develop in two related ways. In each case we'll be linking normative language primarily to the concept and reality of the human family. In the one sense we will treat norm in terms of central tendency. This first notion becomes simply the notion of norm as an unqualified quantitative average of occurrences. Thus later in this presentation we'll be treating the family as a norm in terms of its being the average family. The second notion of norm involves a qualitative focus on the family as the family hypothetically is supposed to be and aspires to be. Thus we look at the criterion family. This is the vision of family that informs and motivates the average family to comport itself as it both ought and wants to comport itself in light of its vision of what that family is supposed to be. So here we entertain two notions of the family as a norm; first, the average family in culture and history, and second, the criterion family as the ideal or vision of family on which the average family counts for its guidance in family integrity and in the image of which it hopes for its fulfillment in the future.

We deal now with the assumption that our average family in civilized society derives its family motivation toward integrity and fulfillment from mythologies of family origin and family destiny. These mythologies employ a similar structure no matter how they may be fleshed out and transmitted in family stories and visions. The versions of these mythological stories and visions of the criterion family vary widely. Each variety reflects the larger national or tribal mythology in which the average nuclear family finds its identity. These myths, or ritual stories, point to both an ab origine

119

120

past and to an eschatalogical future, to a "time at the beginning of
time" and to a "time at the end of time."

          The center of meaning in the family myth of origin, which
it may share with millions of other families, usually involves the
commanding significance of ·a paradigmatic parent, a parent to be emu-
lated for his personal behavior whatever the patriarchal or matriar-
chal circumstances may be said to have been. The center of meaning
in the family myth or vision of its eschatalogical consummation usually involves the commanding significance of the circumstances and
conditions of the family. If the hoped-for family consummation situation involves also a reunion with the paradigmatic parent, even
then the vision speaks primarily of the celebration of the family,
in the consummation situation, with the paradigmatic parent. Most
eschatalogical visions assume that in the consummation the imperative
guidance of the parent personage is no longer needed and no longer
needs serve to evoke in the family the moral decisions implicit in
the family's pilgrimage or mission through history. The rules of
the road, as rules, become transcended when the traveler arrives at
his permanent home, as in fact do the rules of the old home he left.

          We look now more closely at the average family making its
way, generation by generation, through the temporal interim of history. Throughout the journey it finds itself proceeding from the
origin-moment of the paradigmatic parent toward the eschatalogical
consummation at the post-historical journey's end. The average family's problem in history centers first in its struggle to survive by
obeying the implications of its origin myth. At the same time the
average family struggles to succeed toward accomplishing for itself
those conditions its members see to be teleologically attuned to the
consummation. Moral decisions arise from those frequent dilemmas
where so often families find themselves in circumstances where obedience to the "grand parentage" implies present failure to achieve,
or, conversely, where achievement implies a risky disobedience to the
spirit of the patriarchal paradigm. Let me review now three familiar
examples of such mythologies and visions that give major context to
our problem of enlightenment, socialization and emancipation in relation to religion studies in public education. We take them in their
sequence of historical occurrence.

          The great tribal nation of Israel tends historically to de-
rive its mythology of Hebraic origin from the mythological legends of
Abraham and Abraham's god. As a nation it counts its original out-
burst from its prehistory in the times of Moses and Exodus-Sinai.
However even in the life and times of Moses' people in the wilderness
the tribes of Israel felt the paradigmatic imperative of Abraham's
obedience, in faith, to the transcendently faithful justice and guidance of Yahweh. As for the eschatalogical consummation of Israel's
history, the vision involves God's providential arrangement of history in such a way that in the end Israel will live secure and honor-
ed by all nations in aeternum in her own promised land. Every average family of Israel, in the language of Jewish religion, remembers
the original faith of the wandering Aramaean and looks forward to its
place in the final consummation of Israel.

As for the Christian Church, its people persistently derive their mythology of origin from the paradigmatic person of Jesus. Counting his faith as their faith and themselves the beneficiaries of his unique works as the messianic lord, their average family way through history consolidates the Christians in their common calling to the gospel mission to proclaim Christ's salvific lordship. They seek to convert the world, or as much of it as they can, to a similar identification with Christ and to the common good news mission of the Church. It is true that Christian identity comes, according to their doctrine, by virtue of initiatory baptism and not by birthright. However through the long centuries of Christian experience one sees a tendency toward regression to ethnicity. This becomes manifest in the practice of infant baptism and dedication, enhancing the notion of an ethnically oriented, familial Christian genealogy. These Christian family processions through history occur in part as gospel missions, but primarily, it would appear, in these latter days as family pilgrimages. They still persist in their explicit faith in the paradigmatic Christ. They look forward eschatalogically to the consummation of the Church in a post-historical celebration in the presence of the triune God involving a grand reunion with the regnant Christ.

Not all religious communities are primarily theocentric as in the case of the Jews and Christians. I offer the religion of America as an example of religion in which theocentricity is secondary to the central emphasis. Here the paradigmatic parent is both individual and corporate in the persons of George Washington, "the father of his country," and those grouped with him as his associated founding fathers. Patriotic, that is, religiously zealous Americans, revere the mythological legends of these men. They draw upon their deeds for inspiring examples of faith in the national vision of consummation and of loyal American citizenship in the meantime. The average American family looks upon the Stars and Stripes in a manner similar to that in which the average Christian family regards the Cross, or the Jewish family the Star of David. It also looks forward to its American consummation in an eschatalogical future in which a final and permanent American condition will fulfill the family in its status as a primary locus of a great American brotherhood of democracy. It promises to be an America incorruptible in its virtue, impregnable in its strength as the greatest of the nations, and irresistible in its benign influence on the lesser sister nations of the world. In that great American consummation the average family will coequally with all the rest celebrate that eternal vitality and righteousness taught ab origine by the fathers and learned progressively through history by their American posterity.

In all its cultural manifestations the family as average family becomes identified with the historical nuclear family. The average family is the missionary or pilgrim family on the way from its origin to its destiny, on its way from the eternal moment of its original identifying parent-event to the eternal moment of its consummation. Its life inheres in history in this moving process. To the degree that the family sees itself thus immersed in history, and in history's inherent dilemmas, the family will deal with matters of enlightenment, socialization and emancipation as problematic themes and processes. To the extent that the family entertains a vision of itself in terms of obedience to its patriarchal paradigm and in terms

of its aspirations toward its consummatory paradigm, it identifies
itself with the criterion family. The average family seeks enlightenment primarily from the criterion past and for emancipation primarily from the criterion future. For socialization, the process of
current integrity, it struggles to maximize its own responsibility
and ability to receive and achieve a growing measure of knowledge
(enlightenment) and freedom (emancipation) in the concrete life of
the current generation. In all this, then, the criterion past suggests obedience and enlightenment while the criterion future suggests
achievement and freedom. Some families become more involved with
the criterion of origin and gain reputation for their conservatism.
Others become more involved with the criterion of consummation and
earn a reputation for progressivism.

These paradigms that inform the visions of the criterion
family are mythological, involving the boundary situation between
history and mystery. Granted the wide variety of appearances, still
one man's original identifying event is exactly like another's in
that each marks the start of a familial history. A corresponding
comment would be appropriate regarding the consummation. The mythological variety comes, and with it the rub, when people ask the who,
how and why questions that bespeak our dealing with the claims and
counter-claims of revelation. Revelation ties the family origin and
eschaton together in actu in a sacramental present through which is
manifest the presence of both origin and eschaton to the family here
and now. Those of us who live in this moving, memorable moment of
revelation, this history, take both sorrow and delight in it. We
suffer sorrow in that we do not remain obedient to the patriarchal
origin, or, at other times we delight that we do. At still other
times we grieve because we fail to achieve toward the consummation,
and then again we rejoice because we do.

In Jewish tradition enlightenment, socialization and emancipation take form in the revelation language of learning the scriptures, of yearning toward the finally secure and prosperous tribal
home, and of earning the reality of that consummation in the current
events of family obedience to Torah and family achievement in accomplishing one more step along the way. With the learning comes enlightenment, with the earning comes socialization, and, as the consequence of both, the yearning becomes transformed into an earnest-
moment of freedom on loan from the future consummation, the final
emancipation.

Similarly in Christian Church tradition the three processes
of our concern derive their reality from the revelation language of
the Old and New Testaments as the Christians learn it. This spells
enlightenment. Christians abide in Christ as new creatures born a-
gain by grace in faith. They live with lives centered in the cultic
discipline of sacramental Christian worship and in the mission of
the Church. This discipline spells socialization. They commonly
anticipate their consummation in the final moment, the resurrection
world of reunion. This is emancipation.

The American national tradition, like all ethnic or eth-
noid traditions, has developed in light of its own peculiar mythology of origin and destiny. In terms of enlightenment, socializa-

tion and emancipation, the American language of revelation suggests
our learning the minds of the founding fathers as the primary source
of enlightenment. It suggests a family by family appropriation of
the American dream of the future as the teleological source of emancipation. It suggests that in the meantime the American family unite
the beginning and the end, the enlightenment and the emancipation, in
the sacramental events of a current national obedience to the fathers
and a continuing national achievement toward the future. This disciplined citizenry bespeaks the family's effective current socialization. The language of American revelation becomes redolent in the
significance of current national events.

These processes of enlightenment, socialization and emancipation, then, appear in history organically linked to the mythologies
of the familial people. They constitute the living complex of familial and interfamilial activity that strives to find and make manifest
in the current moments of history the eternal moments of origin and
consummation.

In the midst of all this extensive context, how can we regard with rational affection the problem of norm in public education
religion studies? How may the public school articulate its affairs
to the mythologies of Israel, of Christendom, of America, to mention
the three we have treated? What do, and what should, the processes
of enlightenment, socialization and emancipation mean to teachers and
students in our public schools? Should the public school serve
strictly the interests of American religion, or should it serve like-
wise the religion of Israel and that of the Christian Church? Can it
avoid serving the interests of any of these mythological communities,
and should it? We retain these questions in mind as we continue.

The average nuclear family, as I have indicated, scarcely
exists as a lone tradition. It finds its place and identity in common with, and in contradistinction to, numerous other families. At
the level of tribal and national activity, families find themselves
commonly involved in social institutions. These common institutional
activities enlist or require the participation of large numbers of
families in common worship, in common learning, in common order, common production and common art. The types of institutions appropriate
to these common activities are: to worship, the church; to learning,
the school; to order, the state; to production, the economy; and to
art, the studio (i.e., the locus of the muses: drama, music, paint-
ing, etc). These institutions provide a means of interfamilial cooperation and specialization of function. As the types of general
social activity at the public and personally abstract level they in
fact reflect patterns of behavior in each family that occur in some
form or other sui generis. Thus a family may be an American family,
its several members citizens in the American state. Its membership
in the institutional state constitutes not a participation in relationships of order found only external to the family, but an investment of the family experience of order, to one degree or another, in
the interfamilial social order of the state. Yet, with or without
the state, the family order would be real as long as the family existed. The point is that the greater institutions are types of organized behavior that all have their prototypes in the domestic life
of the family. And the type, the institution, derives its reality

124

from the prototype in the family. It finds justification for its existence almost solely in its ability to enhance the life-history of
the family in the family experience of enlightenment, socialization
and emancipation.

This all suggests an obligation by institutions to provide
positive general support for the revelation language of the average
family -- support for all the average families in their obedience to
their patriarchal paradigms and in their efforts to accomplish family
conditions that presage their consummations. It also means institutional respect for the variety of criterion family visions that inform and inspire average family life. Offer what it will, and rightly, still no church, no school, no state, no economy, no art can justify the prescriptive imposition of an institutional mythology upon
the domestic life of a family, whether nuclear or extended. Neither
may an institution rightly prohibit the use of any particular mythology in family life. The right role of the institution is that of
servant. It serves not as master but as servant to the interests of
family. The most primitive and perhaps least spectacular entity, the
average family, constitutes the average norm that every institution
must serve. These average families, in their life-histories collec-
tively, also reveal to the institutions the criterion family norms in
light of which each of these institutions must be justified as a servant of enlightenment, socialization and emancipation.

The common activities of family integrity scarcely can exist devoid of a common family sense of Source and faith in that
Source, or Transcendent. The continuing organized recognition of
that Source is what we call worship. Family learning scarcely can
exist without being founded on the common family faith in a family
Source. Nor can the common family order persist without the Source
authority and common lore by which that order is justified. Family
production needs family order for its effective organization. Finally, family art, the clearest evidence of corporate security and
individual freedom, finds its support and inspiration in the whole
complex of family worship, learning, order and production rendered
organic and alive by the family language of eternal Source, past
paradigm and future consummation.

According to the author's view, the public school presents
an example of that institution, the school generally, which serves
specifically the process of family learning. The school derives its
right to exist not from one or another of its sister institutions,
or from any covenant or concordat among them, but from its service
relationship, along with the rest of them, to its prototype, the
learning family, which is inspired in turn by its criterion family
vision -- the family fully informed and learned in its own lore of
source and condition. The school, properly oriented, finds its
roots and its raison d'etre fundamentally in the life of the family.
The school suffers corruption when it becomes understood, especially
from within its own professional community, as an autonomous institution without external responsibility, or as an institution in service to other institutions. It should not deal with students merely
as its own creatures, or as youthful citizens of the state,
or as youthful members of religious communities, or as fledgling
workers in the economy, or as neophyte disciples of the arts.
According to our view here, the school is an institutional locus of

learning with direct and primary lines of relationship to the family. It serves as the place where people go from the family into the world in order that by laborious inquiry they may incorporate into their lives a wiser and deeper information for the family plus a richer understanding of how they may find manifest in their average family life revealing moments of what the human family is supposed to be and aspires to be.

With regard to the study of religion, a study constituting one of the basic fields of learning in human life, I am pleased when I see the school treating seriously and appreciatively the universal dimension of worship in family life, whatever may be the family mythology of Source, origin and consummation. I am not so pleased when I see the school emphasizing the mythology of one religion alive in the school population at the expense of others. Nor do I like to see the schools teaching religion for something other than what it is, whether under the guise of philosophy, or educational theory, or literature, or social studies, or the arts. Most sad of all to see is the frequent subordination of religion studies not to the service of family life, but to the service of the elitist interests of professional clergy, statesmen, educators, industrialists and artists. In short, I believe that religion studies may not rightly be presented or prohibited as a service to church, state, industry or art -- or to the school itself. The family remains the only human group whose welfare should be served directly by studies in religion. All other benefit is spin-off.

The resolution of the problem of norm in public education religion studies appears to me not to be a matter of either/or choices among the processes of enlightenment, socialization and emancipation. The resolution of the problem lies instead in a growing inclination on the part of the school to provide opportunity to the young and not so young family member to find resources of religious knowledge to share with his family out of his school adventures of inquiry and appreciation. In the field of religion studies this means a lively and disciplined inquiry into the myriad of mythologies and revelations by which families of the world conceive their tribal and national histories in living intercourse with tribes and nations not their own and, within the family, with generations not their own.

It falls to the school, in offering religion studies, to offer enrichment to the student primarily in the way of enlightenment, recognizing with keen sensitivity the close affinity that marks the relationship between worship and learning. The school can do this first by making it quite clear that as an institution it is serving family and not institutional interests as its primary concern. Second, the school can promote the existence of religion studies as a scholarly discipline in its own right. It can demonstrate that religion study courses are not merely a means for taking religion as an object of analysis to enhance the influence of alternative methodologies such as literature, history, sociology or psychology. Third, the school can make it possible for each student to grow in his reverence and curiosity regarding his own religious tradition from which he takes his family identity while at the same time enhancing his knowledge of other mythologies and revelatory languages that inform the histories of families, tribes and nations exotic to

126

his own domestic experience.

It remains for the student and his family to determine what family he does belong to, in what family he will achieve success, in what mythology of family origin and destiny he will experience life while history, the moving moment of revelation, moves him and his fellows to decide and do.

THE PEDAGOGY OF RELIGIOLOGY

Guntram G. Bischoff
Western Michigan University

The study of religion in public schools is no longer new; nor can the casual observer deny that the number of schools offering some opportunity of studying religion is slowly but steadily growing. Nevertheless, there persists in many quarters a certain uneasiness about the whole enterprise. I believe that this uneasiness is not only understandable but justified in view of the ambiguity with which alternatives are stated. It is difficult enough to catch the subtle distinction between "religious studies" and "religion studies," but what is the prospective teacher to say when those who taught him this distinction seem themselves not quite sure of it? And how is he further to relate religion studies to such equally ambiguous terms as private and public education? The problm is, of course, both a practical and a theoretical one in the sense that clarity in practice feeds on theoretical lucidity. Take, for instance, the currently most popular course title for studying religion at the public school, "the Bible as Literature." I suggest this title is basically a political hence practical title: it is designed to keep religion in while somehow keeping overt demonstrations of religiousness out, thereby satisfying the law of the land. At the same time, the title raises weighty theoretical questions: What definition or concept of religion is implied? Is the subject matter presumably indicated by it adequately related to the phenomenon of religion? What is the relationship between religion and literature? And above all, how does all this relate to pedagogical considerations? What view of the nature, function and purpose of education is presupposed? How does it "fit" with the teacher's and the student's milieu, tradition, and expectations? Etc. In brief, I would assign first priority to the theoretical side of the problem: How, where, and subject to what criteria do, can and should the study of religion and public education meet? As long as the problem posed by the study of religion in the public school is not thought through on this level I see little hope for the clarification of approaches and methods and hence for unambiguous language and purposeful practice.

I.

Attempting to suggest a possible route toward answering my own question, I should like to begin by quoting the stated purpose of the National Council on Religion in Public Education. (Several years old, the NCRPE is a kind of national super organization whose members are themselves national organizations, mostly of religious affiliation.) The stated purpose of the Council is "to provide means for co-operative action among organizations concerned with religion as a constitutionally acceptable and educationally appropriate part of a secular program of public education." The core of this formulation reads, "religion as a part of public education." What is meant here by the term "religion," and what by "public education", and how are we to define the relationship between the two?

It may not be amiss at this point to reflect for a minute on the utility and limitation of definitions. To define means to single out, to distinguish, and to identify. That which is not so separable, distinguishable and identifiable cannot be studied. Definitions are useful because they permit clarification of concepts or problems through testing the adequacy of the theory implied in them. By the same token, definitions are by their very nature of limited use. For they are not only tentative formulations representing stages of inquiry, but in a way artificial in that they tend to separate what really belongs together, isolate a phenomenon out of the fulness of its living relationships, and thus fracture reality.

127

This is also the reason why definitions live in a certain frame of reference outside of which they may be quite meaningless and which itself influences the view of the object being defined. This is not unimportant for the task at hand, for the formulation "religion as a part of public education" refers to a point of view which is not in itself scientific, religious, political, social, or psychological, but specifically pedagogical. Correspondingly, we must seek to approach and define religion as an object of study not primarily in theological, politological, sociological or psychological terms, but in pedagogical terms.

Returning to the NCRPE statement of purpose, I take the term "public education" to mean public school education for the purpose of this paper. (And while acknowledging the limitations of this paper, may I add that when referring to the public school I have in mind particularly the upper grades of high school.) Since religious practice in public schools is clearly ruled out of order by Supreme Court decision, the term "religion" can only refer to the study of religion. The phrase, "secular program of public education" is, of course, borrowed from the Schempp decision. Its intent is clearly to qualify the public school and its education as secular. The key element of the sentence, then, is concerned with a particular form of the study of religion which is consistent with secular public school education.

If this interpretation is correct, it implies that the criterion for the proper form of the study of religion is a specific educational one, viz., education as understood with reference to the public school. Hence a viable theory of the study of religion in public schools should be derived from the public school and its education. It should not be deduced from other educational institutions and the educational theory inspiring and informing them, nor may it be derived from religious, political, ethnic or otherwise defined groups and institutions and their respective views of education. The case for the study of religion in the public school cannot be successfully argued unless it can be shown that such study is called for by the very principles on which public school education rests and in terms of which its didactic objectives are conceived.

The result of these preliminary considerations determines the further sequence of my reflections. I will, first, seek to broadly define the objectives of public school education. Next, I will try to identify the kind of study of religion commensurate with these objectives. Finally, I will attempt to extrapolate from these premises some didactic considerations.

II.

1. This is obviously not the place to develop a theory of the public school. I should, however, pause briefly to acknowledge the specific public character of this school since this is of significance for the course of my argument.

The public school reflects a pluralistic society and culture. It is the school for all young citizens. This is another way of saying the public school is "secular" since pluralism itself, as the historical result of the secularization process, constitutes the signature of secularity. By "public" we usually mean that cluster of social obligations, privileges, institutions and activities agreed to be vital to society as a whole, hence common to all of its segments, and opposed to that which is partial and private. The public school, therefore, exists and operates on premises and for purposes established, sustained, and defined by consensus and codified in law.

I am not interested here in the dynamics of consensus, its range or its durability. Rather, I am interested in the very structure of consensus which pre-

cludes at least in principle if not in practice, the ideologization of the public
school in as much as it is the nature of ideologies to be associated with certain
segments of society. It would seem to follow that the public school, if true to
itself as the child of consensus, will not only be ideologically neutral, but that
it will actively and critically cultivate this neutrality. That is to say, the
public school, while necessarily mirroring the pluralistic society to which it owes
its existence, will reflect this pluralism, its origin, its constituent parts, and
its implications, critically. At pain of becoming a "private" school by definition,
it may not become an ideological school of any hue, whether secularistic, religious,
political, social, or otherwise.

It is for these reasons that I do not think that a theory of public school
education can be devolved from particular normative educational ideals since such
ideals are invariably ideologically rooted. Such a theory should rather be developed on the basis of possible and limited consensus as to the broad didactic objectives
of public school education.

2. If we may define education generally as a process enabling a person to autono-
mously order his environment and himself into a meaningful world, and to relate himself to this world in a responsible way, we may define the primary educational objective of the public school as the enabling process which helps develop the young
person's world-understanding and self-understanding. In order that such understanding does not remain heteronomous, but supply the building blocks of the student's
own construction of an experiential cosmos of meaning, world-understanding and self-
understanding must be related not only to the order of fact, but equally to the
order of meaning which is to be constantly tested, regained, and reaffirmed by interpretation, decision, and responsible action.

When speaking of world-understanding, I refer to both the world of nature
and the world of culture. Through the curricular elements relating to the natural
sciences, the student is introduced to the world of natural phenomena. This introduction, I would think, will mostly remain in the order of fact. More difficult is
the student's initiation into the complex world of culture, for here the orders of
fact and meaning are inextricably interwoven. The curricular elements relating to
the social sciences, the humanities, and the arts are particularly charged with the
accomplishment of this task. Mere information however, is not enough in either
case. If the student is to be enabled to responsibly relate himself to the world in
which he lives, he must learn to properly "handle" the information of the data by
becoming familiar with the use of proper methods. The prerequisite medium for methodical understanding in the natural sciences is mathematics. In the cultural
sciences it is primarily language.

Turning to the objective of achieving self-understanding, we may quickly
pass over those aspects, biological and social, which relate solely to the order of
fact. As referent sciences could be mentioned anatomy, genetics, physical anthropology, etc. Again the aspects relating to the order of meaning are patently more
important since without them the young person's growth in self-understanding is impossible and no meaningfully ordered world can arise for him, i.e., no world which
he can accept and affirm as his own. Hence the student must learn to become critically aware of his attitudes, affections, convictions, beliefs, doubts, motives for decision and action, values, judgments and prejudices. Most, if not all, of these are
mediated to him through the self-understanding of other human beings, individuals or
groups, past and present, and therefore require methodical interpretation for adequate understanding. The student encounters the self-understanding of others in
many forms and expressions, but particularly in literature, art, philosophical and

ethical systems, and religion.

By understanding the meaning structures underlying the self-understanding of others, the student is enabled to more fully understand himself, to consciously place himself as it were in the natural and cultural worlds in which he finds himself experientially. This process requires first of all understanding through methodical interpretation. Beyond that, it requires also conscious decision making. While the public school must be careful not to prejudge the student's decision as to the validity of any given meaning structures for himself, it can and should enable and encourage the student to make such decision by himself and for himself. It is the business of the pedagogy of any particular field of inquiry to find out how this is best accomplished with reference to that particular subject matter. May it suffice here to emphasize that, regardless of the details, the student should be exposed to the self-understanding of others in such a way as to render their various claims to meaning-giving truth and value as genuine possibilities for himself which he might wish to adopt for himself and with which he might want to identify himself.

III.

1. Every subject studied in the public school has a referent science among the academic disciplines. For instance, the referent sciences for the school subject of social studies are sociology, social psychology, psychology, history, political science, etc. Now, it is obvious that the social sciences cannot be studied at the public school in the same manner as at the university or by social scientists. Thus it falls to the pedagogy of the social sciences as a separate discipline to seek answers to the questions of what should be studied in a particular educational situation with reference to the social sciences, and why and how such study should be conducted. The place of the pedagogy of the social sciences is between that of the bundle of academic disciplines called social sciences and the general educational sciences. Identical with neither, it is the bridge between both. It is, as it were, the home discipline of the teaching profession. Where does the study of religion fit into this picture?

Our first question should be: What is the proper referent science for the study of religion in the public school? The answer to this question will be of considerable consequence for the construction of an academic pedagogy of religion and for the actual practice of the study of religion in the classroom. This answer cannot be in doubt, however, if we grant the secular character of the public school and its corresponding educational objectives. The referent science of the study of religion in the public school cannot be theology, but solely that bundle of academic disciplines dealing with the various aspects of the phenomenon of religion which is variously referred to as religion studies, or the science of religion, and which I will simply call religiology in order to clearly distinguish it from theology.

If we want to define religiology, it is necessary to bear in mind that it is, first, a "science," and, secondly, that like many sciences it deals with a complex phenomenon. (I put the word "science" in quotation marks in order to signal that I regard not only the natural and social sciences as science, but equally the humanities.) As a science, religiology is characterized by the scientific point of view, that is, it deals logically and critically with empirically available hence observable and verifiable data. Religion is seen as a human phenomenon, and the religious experience as a human experience. The transcendent gods who are typically the content of this experience are empirically available only as part of this experience, not as existing outside of and independent from this experience. Hence transcendence must appear as immanence, as the understanding of the gods must appear as self-understanding. This implies also that questions about the reality of the gods are bracketed by religiology as lying outside the purview of its quest, quite regardless of the personal convictions of the religiologian who may be a believer, an agnostic, or even an atheist. Whether the communicated content of the religious experience is in fact related to another, empirically unavailable, "higher," "supernatural," or "transcendent" reality, and, if so, how this relationship is to be conceived and defined -- these questions are the proper business of theology which affirms the first and seeks to answer the second question. However, it is important to note that in affirming transcendent reality and explaining its relationship to empirical reality, theology itself becomes a religious phenomenon and hence an object of religiology.

We might characterize the relationship between religiology and theology then, as one of mutual limitation as to each one's horizon of perception. Whereas religiology is methodologically a-religious both in structure and intent, theology is religious; whereas religiology is descriptive in intent, theology is normative. Thus it is precisely the non-normative character of religiology that makes it suitable to be the referent science of the study of religion in the non-normative and non-ideological public school.

2. We said that like many other sciences, religiology deals with a complex phenomenon which embraces a number of different aspects or dimensions. Correspondingly, we find a number of independent disciplines focusing on these aspects as well as a number of approaches aimed at their elucidation. We may mention such as the sociological, socio-psychological, psychological, psychoanalytical, historical, philosophical, philological, political, comparative, and pedagogical. That is to say, religiology is not a homogeneous discipline with a single, clearly defined method, but a heterogeneous field of inquiry in which the question of adequate research methodologies is controversial among the participating disciplines.

I should like to mention just one, though perhaps the most important one, of these controversies. I am referring to the question of whether a functional or a substantive definition or approach is more adequate to the explanation of the phenomenon of religion. Please note that the alternative is not that of science vs. some other form of mental activity, but that of two fundamentally different approaches within science, viz., the positivistic and the humanistic, the analytical and the hermeneutical. Functionalism in religiology is criticized by those favoring a substantive definition because it reduces the question of what religion is to the question of how it works. Similarly, the question of the specific content of the religious experience is reduced to the behavior of religious persons.

Let me cite a couple of concrete examples. Most of us are familiar with the popular surge of studying the bible as literature, as part of the study of religion in public schools. In most cases, such study may be taken to imply a functionalist view of the bible. The fact that the bible functions as literature cannot be denied, but does this mean that it is essentially literature like other literature? Again, noone will deny that the bible is also a literary phenomenon permitting and in fact demanding the analysis and interpretation of literary genres and structures. However, the intentionality of the bible is not literary, but religious. To study the bible solely as literature begs the question of what exactly it is that makes religious literature religious. By the same token, the bible's primary effect is that people have in the past and do now believe it, live by it, and value it in a way fundamentally different from the way in which the same people believe, live by, and value other literature including that inspired by the bible. What is at stake is the self-understanding of the bible and its authors, and this can only be found through application of the hermeneutical method.

My second example is taken from a set of state-approved goals for teaching

132

about religion in the public schools of California which includes the following pro-
visions.

> "Students should develop an informed understanding and appreciation of the role
> of religion in the lives of Americans and the people of other nations;"
> "Students should be able to recognize and discuss the influence of religious
> views and values on the social, economic, and political aspects of society;"
> "Students should understand the influence of religion on the development of
> ideas in Western and Eastern cultures and civilizations;"
> "Students should be aware of the influence of religion on lifestyles (such as
> work, prayer, devotion, ritual, worship and meditation);"
> "Students should appreciate problems of conscience in relation to historical
> and contemporary issues of religious freedom."

I submit that the view underlying these goals is indeed a functionalist one. We
hear a great deal about what religion does, how it functions socially and psycholo-
gically, how it has shaped the world of ideas as well as national cultures, music,
literature, and art, and what its historical and contemporary influences are. In
brief, we hear a great deal _about_ religion, but nothing _of_ religion. It is like
studying a house from all sides without ever being permitted to enter it.

The functional approach has dominated the social sciences in this country
almost exclusively for the past decades. There are, however, increasing signs, not
least in the sociology of religion, that this methodological monopoly is being bro-
ken in favor of the search for substantive definitions of religion and a renewed
interest in the phenomenological and hermeneutical approaches to religious phenomena
in which the accent is placed on the empathetic understanding of their essential
identity and their interpretation in terms of the essential structures of the religious experience. This development is of obvious importance to the pedagogy of
religiology; for not only does it reopen the problem of meaning and meaning structures, but it would seem to coincide with the educational importance of the student's
self-understanding.

IV.

1. Turning now to the third and last problem, my chief question is this: Given the
secular character of the public school, hence the scientific tenor of its instruction and its educational objectives, how may we construct an adequate didactic theory
of the study of religion in the public school? Concretely: How, and in which ways
can the study of religion oriented toward religiology contribute to the student's
growth in world-understanding and self-understanding?

The answer would seem easiest with regard to world-understanding, for once
we are willing to abandon a purely positivist approach to the phenomenon of religion,
it becomes clear that no human culture is intelligible without the religious dimension. As I have argued earlier, the question is not that of a normative methodology.
On the contrary, the desired objective of the student's growth toward autonomous
understanding -- that is, his progressive emancipation from the tutelage of the
teacher's sheer authority -- requires that he be initiated to all contending metholo-
gies so as to become aware of the possibility of approaching the phenomenon of religion in different ways leading to different conclusions.

When I, nonetheless, argue in favor of giving preference to the historical-
hermeneutical approach, I do so mainly for didactic reasons. The presentation of
religious data in the school will be largely tied to texts, the interpretation of
which requires the hermeneutical method. Moreover, while the student already has

ample occasion to use the empirical-analytical approach in other subject areas, he
has at present little, if any, opportunity to become familiar with the hermeneutical
method. The emphasis on the religious phenomenon per se should not be taken, however, to imply the neglect of its interrelatedness with other cultural phenomena,
and for the study of these relationships functional descriptions as well as socio-
critical evaluations are at least as appropriate as hermeneutical analyses. No autonomous world-view can be achieved in a pluralistic society without critique, and I
firmly believe that the all-too frequent call for an uncritical treatment of religious phenomena -- hidden under the cloak of pseudo-objectivity -- is fundamentally dishonest and an affront to the intellectual and moral integrity of the student
as well as of the teacher.

2. Moving on to the development of the student's self-understanding, it may well be
said that here the study of religion comes into its own. At least from the didactic
point of view, this is the central place of such study in the public school curriculum. (I should like to observe in passing that while certain ingredients of the
study of religion necessary to the building of the student's world-understanding
could, perhaps, be integrated successfully into other, existing subject areas, such
as literature and history, the full achievement of the objective of self-understanding would seem to call for separate treatment of such subjects as religion, philosophy, and ethics.)

        The task posed by the student's need to grow in self-understanding specifi-
cally demands the hermeneutical approach. Functionalist explanations as well as
phenomenological descriptions of religious phenomena are not very helpful in this,
for at stake is the conscious confrontation of the student with the claim or claims
which the self-understanding of others exerts on him. The mere fact of such claims
is unavoidable. Since a young person's self-interpretation is itself a social process, it inevitably depends on the self-understanding of other human beings, particularly those who have shaped his own tradition. The only and crucial alternative
is therefore, whether the student is to become the victim of the self-understanding
of others, interiorizing it by default, or whether he will be enabled through critical reflection to arrive at responsible decision.

        If we now may define religion formally as the effective unity of ultimate-
ly posited values and meanings, expressed objectively in historically grown religions
and subjectively in religious individuals; and if further we may define self-understanding as life-affirmation of the personal center, or that goal-image of a person's
self toward the realization of which he employs the creative and voluntary powers of
his life -- it becomes all-important that the various historical and contemporary
claims to meaning-giving truth and value confront the student authentically, that
is, as genuine possibilities for the formation of his own goal-image.

        In a recent article published in Religious Education, Br. Gabriel Moran
decries the present dilemma of religious education apparently having no other choice
but that between proselytisation by ecclesiastical institutions and "antiseptic observation." By the latter term he means "religious study which in reaction to the
Churches pretends to total neutrality and scientific objectivity." Now, Br. Moran
may be forgiven for looking at religiology through the eyes of a theologian and thus
confusing its internal excitement with the dullness which ensues in the churches'
use of it which he rightly feels to be an escape from their specifically religious
task. Educationally speaking, however, Br. Moran is absolutely right. If the study
of religion in the public school were indeed nothing more than "antiseptic observation," such study would be quite worthless, indeed detrimental to the growth in self-
understanding, and thus irreconcilable with the didactic objectives of public school
education.

134

It may be objected that this call for the student's personal engagement
plunges us into a dilemma in that it posits necessary, but illegitimate means for
the achievement of legitimate objectives, at least with regard to the study of religion. I am referring, of course, to the Supreme Court's use of such formulations
as "objective study" and "study about religion." I do not think the objection holds.
As I have stated earlier, it is an essential part of the educational requirement of
growth toward autonomy that the public school refrain from making decisions for, and
on behalf of the student. Concomitantly, I would argue that the confrontation necessary for the student's self-interpretation is made possible precisely through objective study, and that, in fact, authenticity presupposes objectivity. The self-
understanding implicit in religious phenomena -- say, a surah of the Qur'an -- is
not available other than through methodical interpretation, i.e., through the application of the critical canons of the hermeneutical method. Such self-understanding is presented objectively only if and when its authentic claim is allowed to shine
through the interpretation. Proselytizing cannot achieve this because its interpretation is uncritical; mere "antiseptic description" cannot achieve it because it
does not interpret at all, hence is not experientially related. Neither will lead
the student to risk anything, but such risking of his inchoate self-interpretation
and pre-judgments is indispensible if he is to grow toward autonomy and if he is to
reach that threshold of decision beyond which he is on his own. In this sense the
study of religion is, strictly speaking, propaedeutical to the student's own theo-
logizing. Under no circumstances should the student be shielded from a theological
as any other religious claim out of a mistaken fear or sense of objectivity. Such
however well-intentioned protectivity would only shortchange the student's right to
know and indeed make genuine self-understanding impossible.

V.

In conclusion, I should like to summarize by formulating six theses.

1. The rationale and the didactic principles of the study of religion in the public
school are to be derived exclusively from the theory of the public school and its
educational objectives.

2. The task of reflecting this criterion and its implications for the study of religion in the public school, as also the orientation of such study to its referent
science of religiology, is properly lodged with the discipline of the pedagogy of
religiology.

3. Starting with the clear distinction between the study of religion in public schools
and religious instruction in private religious communities, such distinction should
be repeated on the level of pedagogical reflection between the pedagogy of religiology and religious education, as well as on the level of their respective referent disciplines, between religiology and theology.

4. The study of religion should be an integral part of public school curricula since
the educational objectives of the public school prominently include the student's
development of autonomous world-understanding and self-understanding, and because the
study of religion is an important element in both.

5. The study of religion in the public school should emphasize the hermeneutical
method as the method most adequate to the interpretation of the self-understanding of
historically grown religions as well as religious individuals. However, such emphasis should not be to the exclusion of other methods and approaches.

6. The study of religion in the public school should issue in the objective confrontation of the student with the authentic claim to ultimate value and meaning implicit in the religious phenomena studied and thus fully engage the student by enabling him to come to an informed decision as to their relevancy and validity for himself.